RYDE'S HERITAGE
OUR TOWN, YOUR HISTORIES

RYDE SOCIAL HERITAGE GROUP

Acknowledgements

In developing, researching and presenting the various aspects of Ryde's past, Ryde Social Heritage Group (RSHG) has worked with a number of people, groups and agencies, and the Committee of RSHG would like to thank:

Sally-Ann Garrett; Ryde Development Trust; Isle of Wight Council Bereavement Services Department; advisers from the Local Heritage Initiative and the Heritage Lottery Fund; all the staff at the Isle of Wight Record Office; staff and volunteers at The George Street Centre; Isle of Wight Natural History Society; Isle of Wight Family History Society; Isle of Wight PC Users Group; National Federation of Cemetery Friends; The Footprint Trust; Mark Stallard Transport; Clancy Docwra (IoW); Matrix e-Business; Al Rowe (The Potting Shed Man); all the individuals who have given us information, stories, memories or artefacts; Roy Brinton - Honorary President of RSHG; all Members of RSHG for their continuing support, and particularly those who have taken an active role and have worked so hard to bring this publication to fruition.

Disclaimer

This book is not or intended to be a complete history of Ryde and its people. We are aware the chapters do not include, for example, all the churches and places of worship or all the schools we know to exist or have existed in the town or all the maritime and transport stories, but do include some of the ones Ryde Social Heritage Group members have been able to research to date. There are many more histories and stories waiting for RSHG members to discover in the coming months and years for future publications.

Dedication

This book is dedicated to the memory of Les Barrett, a founding member of Ryde Social Heritage Group, a lovely man who, with his wife Ann, spent many, many hours in the Isle of Wight Record Office, reading fiche, film, and paper records, to gather together the tales from the past that were originally published in the newspapers of the day, and in the archive materials. Sadly, Les passed away before he could see the result of his labours and the publication of Ryde's Heritage: Our Town, Your Histories, but the Group will not forget the huge contribution he made to enable us to share with you the stories of the people of Ryde. Ann continues this work, and we are eternally grateful for the contribution made by this generous couple.

CONTENTS

CHAPTER 1

INTRODUCTION

This book is the culmination of activities carried out by Ryde Social Heritage Group (RSHG) between March 2002 and April 2008. One of the Group's objectives is to research and promote the sharing of information about the history of the town of Ryde on the Isle of Wight. Much of our work is based in Ryde Cemetery where we are producing plot maps and transcribing the memorial inscriptions. We are researching the lives and deaths of some of the people buried there.

We are proud to present the outcome of more than five years of work – the first time such a range of information has been drawn together.

Ryde Cemetery is owned and maintained by the Isle of Wight Council, Bereavement Services Section, and covers about 12 acres of land with access, at the present time (2008) only from West Street. Individual headstones and memorials are the responsibility of the people who purchased the plots.

The cemetery developed on ancient fields and meadowland and has never been subjected to the use of intensive modern farming practices or the use of herbicides and chemicals. It contains a rich heritage of plants and animals that find a haven in the urban centre of Ryde. RSHG has photographed and recorded much of the flora and fauna in the cemetery. Some of the findings of the research are recorded on an interpretation board in the cemetery.

The cemetery, like many others across the country, provides a rich source of social history and is one of the important starting points for researching local history, events, and social development within the area. It holds the key to nearly all aspects of the town's development over the last 160 years – founding families, famous and infamous residents, soldiers lost in the many wars, social figures, and local families still resident today.

RSHG started by transcribing information from the fast eroding memorial inscriptions in the cemetery, then researching any information available on the individuals mentioned on the memorials. Results of this research are recorded on RSHG website, www.rshg.org.uk enabling it to be preserved and accessible to as many people as possible.

Local Heritage Initiative Grant

RSHG applied to the Local Heritage Initiative (LHI), and in August 2005, received a grant of nearly £25,000 for a project lasting two and half years. This funding helped to pay for the development of RSHG website www.rshg.org.uk, a number of exhibitions, the publication of this book and other publications to assist children and adults studying the history of Ryde.

The Local Heritage Initiative was a partnership between the Heritage Lottery Fund, Nationwide Building Society, and the Countryside Agency, and the funding has enabled the Group to establish and share a rich source of information about Ryde's heritage. When the Local Heritage Initiative closed in March 2007, overseeing of the project was handed over to the Heritage Lottery Fund.

The exhibitions held in local, accessible venues, presented and displayed some of the results of the Group's research, including photographs and stories about the people, businesses and development of the town. We have also given illustrated talks to other special interest groups to publicise the work of Ryde Social Heritage Group.

Development of the website has included the introduction of a searchable database. This allows researchers visiting the website to easily search for names of interest and it will allow the Group to continue adding and managing records for years to come.

The website, exhibitions and written information have helped local residents find their links to the past, and widened their knowledge and appreciation of local history. Ryde's families have descendants all over the world and, through the website, information is accessible to a worldwide audience of people who may otherwise not be able to enhance their knowledge of their ancestors, or their interest in Ryde.

Ryde Social Heritage Group

RSHG is a group made up of people with an interest in the local history of the town. All work done on behalf of the Group is on a voluntary basis. Members who just want to attend meetings and give the Group moral support are as welcome as those who want to get involved. The Group generally meets quarterly in January, April, July and October. At these meetings, there is usually a presentation on some aspect of the social heritage of Ryde as well as the normal business of the Group.

There is an annual membership fee agreed by the membership at the AGM. For this fee, members receive a quarterly newsletter, called Beyond the Graves, full of stories uncovered by the most recent research, free entry to members' meetings with guest speakers, and voting rights at the AGM, held in or around October each year.

Working Groups for Family History, Mapping, Natural History, Publications, Research, and Transcribing allow members to participate in any aspect of the project that particularly interests them. Some members belong to more than one working group.

Working Groups' activities cover all aspects of the work of RSHG:

- The Mapping Group, led by David Earle has carried out the painstaking surveying in the cemetery and is producing a set of clear plot maps for the cemetery that not only assist the Transcribing Group in their work but also help other people locate graves in the cemetery.

- The Transcribing Group, led by Janette Gregson has spent hours transcribing the graves in the cemetery.

- The Research Group, led by Ann Barrett, has investigated and typed up details of obituaries and funeral reports from old newspapers; found birth and death records, and searched census records for information on the people buried in Ryde Cemetery.

- The Publications Group, led by Carol Strong, has produced Newsletters, posters, booklets, leaflets, and ensured timely publicity in the local press. This group has also been instrumental in the development of this book.

Other areas members might like to become involved in are looking at the Natural History in the cemetery, Family History Research, Schools liaison or helping out with exhibitions or presentations.

RSHG is a member of the National Federation of Cemetery Friends and of the British Association for Local History. These memberships ensure the Group is following local and national guidance for the heritage project about Ryde.

RSHG's website has generated awareness of the Group's activities within the local community on the Isle of Wight, as well as in other regions of the UK, and from all over the world. We have received emails with comments and queries from America, Australia, Canada, New Zealand, South Africa, Malawi and Sweden to name a few.

Without the efforts of RSHG the valuable information based in the cemetery, an irreplaceable part of Ryde's heritage, could be lost to the effects of weather erosion, wear and tear, and the encroachment of nature. Bringing together the information from the cemetery with detailed research about the people and their lives, RSHG has created a resource that is invaluable in ensuring the social heritage of Ryde is available to the greater community.

The Group is keen to get other people enthused and involved in our continuing historical research about Ryde. Why not join Ryde Social Heritage Group, and find out how you can support the work of the Group?

A membership form can be found in the back of this book, or you could contact:

Janette Gregson
Chairperson and Secretary, RSHG
The Cemetery Lodge
63 West Street
Ryde, Isle of Wight
PO33 2QF

David Earle
Membership Secretary, RSHG
Dove Cottage
17 Hope Road
Ryde, Isle of Wight
PO33 1AG

Objectives of RSHG

- To investigate all aspects of the history contained within Ryde Cemeteries
- To promote the heritage of the town of Ryde, Isle of Wight
- To engage the local community in researching their local history
- To host exhibitions and training workshops to support the project
- To produce publications interpreting the heritage of Ryde
- To design and produce an interpretation panel in keeping with the wider regeneration programme interpreting the heritage of Ryde Cemetery
- To publicise activities of the Group in the local media

Activities for the project carried out from September 2005 to May 2008:
- September 2005: press releases issued to the Isle of Wight County Press, the Portsmouth Echo and local radio about the success of the grant application and to publicise the project
- September 2005: an article about the project published in the Ryde Beacon, a magazine delivered free to all households in Ryde
- September to December 2005: meetings of RSHG held on a monthly basis at Ryde Development Trust offices, Union Lane, Ryde
- September to December 2005: the website was developed to create a dynamic database driven site
- November to December 2005: preparations made for the project launch exhibition
- January to December 2006: meetings of RSHG held on a monthly basis, moving from the Ryde Development Trust, Union Road, Ryde, to the George Street Centre as the membership increased
- March 2006: project exhibition held in Ryde, with the launch of the new website
- August 2006: presentation to the Ryde branch of the Isle of Wight Society
- January 2007 onwards: community involvement in continuing research and collation of burial information to record and preserve local history
- January 2007 Members' Meeting with guest speaker Paul Donnellan
- February 2007: Exhibition held in Ryde Library in conjunction with other local history groups
- March 2007: presentation to the Isle of Wight Family History Society

- April 2007: Members Meeting with a presentation on Early Ryde to 1840 given by RSHG Honorary President, Roy Brinton
- July 2007: Members Meeting with a presentation by Richard Smout, Isle of Wight Archivist, on Family History Resources for Ryde
- September 2007: Two Open Days held in Ryde Cemetery on 8 and 9 September in conjunction with National Heritage Open Days with an exhibition and guided walks
- October 2007: AGM and quarterly Members Meeting with presentation by Derek Warman on Michael Maybrick
- January 2008: Members Meeting with a presentation on the History of Oakfield CE Aided Primary School by RSHG member David Earle
- April 2008: Members meeting with a presentation on Ryde Waterworks by Fred Caws
- May 2008: publication of this book, Ryde's Heritage: Our Town, Your Histories and end of project exhibition

LHI

The Lottery Heritage Initiative (LHI) supported community projects with grants of £3,000 to £25,000 for anything from archaeology to oral history, environmental projects, customs and traditions. LHI was a national grant and advice scheme, devised and run by the Countryside Agency on behalf of the Heritage Lottery Fund, and supported by Nationwide Building Society. This unique three-way partnership successfully enabled more than 1200 communities to undertake projects celebrating their local heritage, gain new skills, and develop a greater awareness of the importance of heritage on their doorstep, with the total value of grant awards exceeding £18 million. LHI finished at the end of March 2007, but the work continues under the Heritage Lottery Fund.

CHAPTER 2

THE HISTORY OF RYDE CEMETERY

Snow in February 2004

Morning Shadow September 2006

The History

Ryde Cemetery contains many graves and vaults. They are the last resting place of many well-known Ryde families from the 19th century to the present day.

In September 1840 George Player, lord of the Manor, offered to donate an acre of land in Ryde for a burial ground. The offer was accepted and a rate was raised for enclosing the land. Ryde Cemetery officially opened in 1842 when the chapel on West Street was consecrated. Holloway's Guide of 1848 records the chapel was dedicated to St Paul.

Ryde Cemetery is, in origin, older than any of the other municipal cemeteries on the Island and predates the Burial Act of 1853 by over 10 years (the next oldest municipal cemetery is at Northwood, established in 1856).

The prosperity of many local trades people and businessmen can be seen from the considerable number of imposing and elaborate stone memorials that exist. Some of the wealthiest families purchased sufficient space for construction of vaults where several members of the family could be buried together.

The oldest graves are in the southeast corner of the cemetery. This part of the cemetery is known as the Old Parish Cemetery (OPC) and is shown on the Ryde Town Commissioners' Survey of 1854 to 1855. Some of the earliest graves identified so far by Ryde Social Heritage Group include those of Charles Saunders, Mary Ann Osmond, Lawrence Brown, Thomas Murray, Harriet Chester, Henry Groves, Sarah Price, John Wagner and Emma Cooper.

Lawrence Brown memorial

John Wagner memorial

The first documented meeting of the Cemetery Committee was held on 28 October 1858. Members of the Committee were made up from the Town Commissioners: Benjamin Barrow, Edward Thurlow (appointed Chairman), William Gabell, Joseph Futcher, Thomas Dashwood and George Riddett.

On 11 January 1859, the Commissioners were constituted as a Burial Board and they approached Estate owners in Ryde for additional land to use for burial grounds.

In 1860 the Secretary of State recommended meetings and proceedings of the Burial Board should be held and kept separate and distinct from the meetings of the Town Commissioners.

The first meeting of the new separate Burial Board was on 28 February 1860. Present were: George Riddett (Chair), William Gabell, William Stratton, James Fairall, James Littlefield, William Gibbs, William Cox, James Harbour, John Stannard, William Cutler, Matthew Newman, Edward Thurlow, George Oakley, John M Jolliffe, Thomas Dennis, Joseph Futcher, John Harbour, Robert Baker, Thomas Hellyer, James Colenut, Henry Hillier, Shem Comden, Charles Dimmick and James Williams, (24 men).

The meeting considered offers of land for the proposed new cemetery:
a) From the owners of the Player Estate, about 4 acres for enlarging the present cemetery at £250 per acre; land to the north and west of the present cemetery, with space for a vault for the Player family.
b) From Sir Henry Oglander, 10 acres of the north part of Smallbrook Farm at £50 per acre.
c) From Sir John Simeon, Bart, about 14 acres forming part of St John's Estate on the south side of Oakfield at a rent of £25 per annum, or £600 purchase.

After a vote, it was decided to extend the present cemetery on the land offered by the Player Estate. On 14 May 1860, Mr Gabell suggested an amendment saying three acres of land were sufficient for the requirements of the town and "the interment of the dead in such close proximity to the living is dangerous to the health". The amendment was not carried: 13 votes were cast for the original proposal, 3 for the amendment and 1 neutral.

The Surveyor's Certificate from Francis Newman, Town Surveyor confirmed the land could be effectively drained:
"I hereby certify that the proposed site for a new cemetery adjacent to the present burying ground, can be efficiently drained in the High Street sewer, by placing a drain at the west end of Hill Street, 20 feet below the surface. The length of the drain from the lowest point of the land to the main sewer will be 499 yards."

The Committee recommended an estimate be obtained to enclose the burial ground with a stone wall and provide necessary chapel accommodation, drainage, roads, footpaths, and planting in order that an application could be made to Her Majesty's Treasurer for the power to borrow the money required.

An estimate for the works was received from J Newman:

- Main drain from lower end of Hill Street to western side of the cemetery of stoneware pipes; the branch drains of agricultural pipes 8 feet below the surface: £380.
- Enhance roadway, roads, and footpaths by raising ground at the northwest corner, lowering that next to the sandpit, and partially filling the pit: £270.
- Stone Boundary wall, 5 feet high above the surface with pair of entrance gates, arched gateway and foot gate (materials from north and west walls of the old cemetery allowed for in this estimate): £340.
- Planting: £50
- Cost of the chapels, lodge and mortuary house necessarily depends on their size as well as the architectural character but buildings equal to those usually found in cemeteries of this size for the following sums:
  - Episcopal and Dissenters chapels with porches and robing rooms, connected by an Archway (allowance is made in this estimate for the materials of the old chapel): £800.
  - Lodge with tool house: £200
  - Mortuary House: £50

The total estimate was £2090.

Tenders for the total work of building the chapels, laying out drains and roads, and building the walls were received in September 1861 from:

- Thomas Sibley, Ryde: £1449
- Thomas R White, Landport: £1450
- James Grimes, Southsea: £1492-17s-1d
- Thomas Dashwood, Ryde: £1587
- James and John Langdon, Ryde: £1700
- John Meader, Ryde: £1700
- James Colenutt, Ryde: £1727
- Josiah Cutler, Ryde, £1893-9s-10d
- Joseph Chapell, Ryde: £1935
- James Smith & William Jackman, Ryde: £1940

Following discussions and a vote, Thomas Sibley's estimate for the work was accepted in October 1861.

An extension to the OPC was made to the north and west and included building of the two central chapels, one being Church of England and the other Nonconformist. The original chapel to St Paul on West Street later became the town mortuary.

A Burial Rate of two pence in the pound was levied in August 1862. In September, estimates were requested for trenching, levelling, seeding and planting, of around £150. James Hellyer was appointed as collector of the burial rates, at a salary of £10 per year, and a bond of £100.

The Clerk was directed to apply to the Superintendent of Police for three policemen to attend the Ceremony of Consecration and the Town Crier be directed to attend in uniform, and have charge of the keys of the Chapels.

Rev Charles Richard, Bishop of Winchester, consecrated the ground and chapel on 28 November 1862 at 1:30pm; the southern portion was consecrated for Church of England rites; the northern portion and chapel left un-consecrated "for any duly authorised or recognised Minister or preacher of any Christian congregation".

A portion of the cemetery was set apart for the burial of Roman Catholics. Rev J Telford requested permission to erect a cross in the centre of the land and to place seats and border tiles, and small boundary stones at the angles.

Applications for the post of Cemetery Superintendent were received from
- Frederick Fountain, 45, Sandown, road surveyor
- George Reid, 26, Ryde, gardener
- Joseph Warder, 31, Ryde, station master
- Thomas Guy, 32, Ryde, labourer
- James James, 27, Ryde, gardener
- Henry Import, 60, Oakfield, gardener
- James Elias Sellars, 37, Ryde, labourer
- James Whitney, 32, Ryde, gardener
- John Salter, 38, Ryde, gardener
- George Robins, 40, Bath chairman

A vote was taken on 5 December 1862 and Henry Import was selected by ballot. His weekly wage was to be £1 until the Lodge was erected and afterwards 17s per week.

Tenders for building the Lodge were submitted by:
- Thomas Sibley, Ryde, £333
- James Smith, Ryde, £375
- John Denham, £330

- James Colenutt, £322
- John Meader, £299

John Meader's tender was selected, his being the lowest amount.
Henry Import took possession of the Lodge on 14 September 1863. The Burial Board provided the following items for his use:

"One armchair, and nine other chairs to be obtained for Lodge, and a table with a drawer, and druggett, an ink stand and roller, Holland blinds to the windows and a seat for outside, with a mat and scraper with fender and irons and hat pegs".

On the 1866 Ordnance Survey map, two central chapels are shown, labelled as 'Episcopal Chapel' and 'Dissenters Chapel'. The original chapel of St Paul on the eastern edge (West Street) of the cemetery is shown as 'Episcopal Chapel (Old)'. The lodge is also on this map.

In August 1866 Henry Import, the superintendent, was reported to be ill. Mr Guy was temporarily employed at £1 per week, to include Sundays; his duties to dig graves in the un-consecrated ground, to "give up all his time to the duties required of him", to employ labour as required to dig graves in the consecrated ground and to keep the chapels clean.

Henry Import died on 22 September 1866. The Committee decided no fee was to be charged for his burial. (RSHG have not yet located his grave and can find no record of his burial at Bereavement Services. It is possible his family did not take up the offer of the free burial and Henry Import is buried in another cemetery).

A ballot was held to select Henry's replacement from the following men:
- Henry Mew, Ryde, gardener
- George Bushell, Haylands, gardener
- Thomas Guy, Ryde, labourer
- Charles Phillbrick, Ryde, gardener
- Henry Butcher, Ryde, gardener
- James White, Southampton, Master of Sailors Home
- Henry Munt, Ryde, gardener

Henry Mew was appointed to commence duties as the second Superintendent on 15 October 1866.

In July 1877, the Burial Board agreed the depth of graves should be eight feet for people interred at the expense of the Parish or Union. This would allow a second burial in the same grave. This is often referred to as an over-burial.

In March 1879, new regulations were drawn up. Headstones were only to be allowed on graves where an exclusive right of burial was purchased, and no bare earth was to be left exposed.

A request in 1880 for the Council to forgo fees for the erection of a monument to the late Superintendent of Police, John Henry Burt, was agreed.

The grave of John Henry Burt is in the Old Cemetery Section O/P plot 2160 on RSHG map RSHG 010 D3.

John Henry Burt memorial

undecipherable first line
was erected by................
of the
Ryde Borough Police Force
in Memory of
Their Late Superintendent
John Henry Burt
Who died 18th June 1880
Aged 45 Years
Be ye also ready for in such an hour as ye think not the
Son of Man Cometh

A large extension to the cemetery was made in 1881, again with land purchased from the Player Estate. This extension to the west took the boundary to Pellhurst Road and today Ryde Cemetery covers almost 12 acres.

Henry Mew memorial

Henry Mew, second Superintendent of the cemetery, died on 24 January 1887 and is buried in the Old Cemetery, Section T Plot 2914 (Double Plot), RSHG Map 020 C2.

His son, William Edward Mew, the Superintendent of Chichester Cemetery, West Sussex, is mentioned on Henry's memorial.

IN
LOVING MEMORY
OF
HENRY MEW
FOR OVER TWENTY YEARS
SUPERINTENDENT OF THIS CEMETERY
WHO PASSED AWAY JAN.24th 1887
"Why should our tears in sorrow flow
When God recalls his own
and bids them leave a world of woe
For an immortal crown"
ALSO OF HIS SON
WILLIAM EDWARD MEW
FOR 37 YEARS SUPERINTENDENT OF CHICHESTER CEMETERY
DIED APRIL 5TH 1928
AGED 87 YEARS
(INTERRED IN CHICHESTER CEMETERY)

The Ordnance Survey map of 1896 shows the extension stretching as far as Pellhurst Road. This map also shows the shelterbelt of conifer trees that still exists along the boundary with Pellhurst Road. By this time, houses had been built on three sides of the cemetery, but land to the south was still occupied by allotments and nurseries.

The consecration of an additional piece of land measuring 1½ acres and containing 1,537 grave spaces took place in October 1906 by the Right Rev Lord Bishop of Southampton.

The report of the ceremony was published in the Isle of Wight Observer dated Saturday 28 October 1906:

"The weather was somewhat threatening at times, but rain held off sufficiently to make the use of a marquee, which had been erected for the occasion, unnecessary. Everyone must have been impressed by the remarkable neat and well-kept appearance of the cemetery, the beautiful situation and environment of which the Bishop deemed worthy of comment.

A complete tour of the ground to be consecrated was made, after which, at a spot facing that portion, the short prayers, preparatory to the act of consecration, were read. Then at the direction of the Bishop, the Registrar read the Articles of Consecration. The latter were signed by the Bishop, who proceeded to deliver a short address.

In conclusion His Lordship expressed his thankfulness that he had been able to perform the ceremony, and hoped that the happy impressions of that day would long continue and constitute an impulse in the hearts of all who had taken part in the service to care for the new ground and do their best to make it beautiful."

By 1939, the revised Ordnance Survey map shows Adelaide Place and the Nurses' Home built to the south of the cemetery, although virtually no change had taken place within the cemetery except for a minor addition to the path network. In 2002, the Nurses' Home was demolished, and houses were built in its grounds.

Design and Layout

The Ordnance Survey map of 1866 shows a central drive running west from the main entrance in West Street (then known as Cemetery Street) to the western end of the cemetery. A turning circle is shown in the centre of the cemetery surrounding the two chapels with another turning circle at the western end of the drive.

The present layout of Ryde Cemetery maintains the central east-west drive with turning circles and a simple parallel grid of paths. The numerous small paths running north-south shown on the Ordnance Survey map are no longer present.

The map also shows the cemetery thickly planted with trees along the north-south paths, the exception is in the southeast corner where fewer trees are shown.

Roman Catholic Memorial Cross

A memorial cross was erected to commemorate the consecration of the land for the burial of Roman Catholics, by Thomas, Bishop of Southwark in 1863.

At the base of the cross is an inscription recording the consecration. This inscription mentions the Roman Catholic portion of the cemetery was marked out by four corner stones, but only one of these has been identified today.

Corner stone

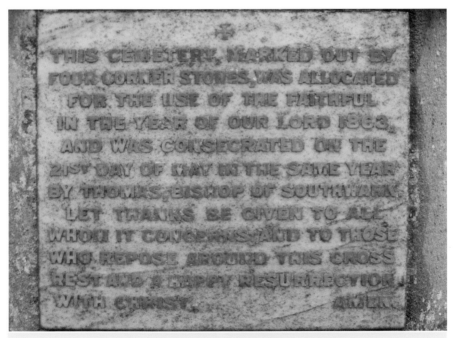

Roman Catholic Memorial Cross Inscription

Buildings and Walls

The main entrance gateway, lodge and central chapels are all built in a similar style and employ similar materials, but the earlier chapel of St Paul, built in about 1842, is of a different construction and style.

This early chapel is situated on the eastern boundary to the south of the later entrance gateway. The east door of the chapel opens directly onto West Street and is set within a two-centred arch of Early English style with dogtooth decoration. Above the door is a double lancet window with quatrefoil tracery.

The building is constructed of roughly shaped stone with corner buttresses to the West Street facade and has a slate roof.

St Paul's Chapel, West Street, Ryde

The entrance gateway is constructed in the polychrome brick, fashionable in the High Victorian period. Here the yellow brick used for the main body of the structure contrasts rather harshly with the two shades of red brick used for the arches and for horizontal banding.

West Street Cemetery Entrance

To the north of the main archway for wheeled traffic is a smaller arch for pedestrians. Both arches have gabled roofs, the main arch being surmounted by a cross.

At right angles to the entrance arch, and immediately north of it, is The Lodge, now in private ownership. This building is of stone with brick quoins and window dressings and a slate roof.

A two storey central projection with gabled roof has three arched entrances at ground level, forming a porch. The lintels over the porch and windows are of the same red brick as used in the entrance gateway and central chapels.

Ryde Cemetery Lodge

The two central chapels are linked by a slate roofed porch with decorative wooden gables. The main drive passes through the central archway and a turning circle surrounds the chapels. There was a bell tower over the porch.

In July 1864, a 2cwt bell was obtained from John Warne and Sons with "as deep a note as possible." The bell tolled slowly at funerals but was removed in 1870 following complaints from some of the neighbours. The tower was taken down some time after that.

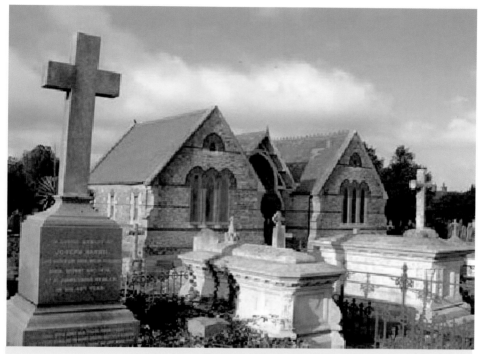

Central Chapels looking eastwards

The two buildings are of identical construction, being of stone with yellow brick quoins and lower window dressings, and horizontal bands of red brick. The eastern facade of each chapel contains a triple lancet window with arches of banded red brick. There is an additional single light in each gable, arched in red-banded brick.

To the west of the twin chapels, and immediately north of the central path, is a small building first shown on the 1896 map and lies at the eastern end of the cemetery extension of 1881.

This building is known as The Bothey, soil store, or gardener's shed. It is a T-shaped structure of stone with yellow brick dressings and tiled gabled roofs with finials. An arched doorway faces south into the cemetery.

The Bothey, Ryde Cemetery

The cemetery is partly surrounded by a wall of Binstead stone from a local quarry. In the southeast corner of the cemetery, the wall is higher than elsewhere along the southern boundary, and this portion of wall is presumed to have been constructed when the first part of the cemetery was laid out.

Ryde Cemetery Wall

CHAPTER 3

RYDE BEGINNINGS AND GROWTH TO 1836

© ROY BRINTON

View of Spithead from Ryde

From the earliest known records and until the 19th century Ryde consisted of two small communities. On the shore was a row of cottages and to the east Ostend Farm. In addition to the cottages, there were at least three inns, a brewhouse and a large malthouse. The inhabitants obtained their livings from the sea, boat building, fishing, ships' pilots and working the passage on the Ryde-Portsmouth route. Lower Ryde could not expand because there was a high bank to the south (where today is Castle Street), a poor shoreline to the west, sandbanks to the east and the sea to the north. In documents this community was known as Ryde Shore or Lower Ryde.

Up the hill, southwards from the shore and separated by the fields called Great Node Close and Little Node Close, was a group of farms known as Ryde Street or Upper Ryde. The inhabitants here obtained their living from the land. The farmsteads faced into the road, which ran north to south (today's High Street). The farmers worked the fields around the steadings leased to them by the lord of the Manor. This was the remnant of a type of medieval farming. Some of the land was unenclosed and it is thought that Sandy Lakes farm was the last to be enclosed in the 17th century (north of Queens Road). It was along Ryde Street that flocks of sheep, which had come from the mainland and unloaded down on the shore, were driven on their way to the downs for summer grazing. From the 17th century there was an inn and some alehouses.

To understand the growth of Ryde there is a need to look at the manorial history, which played such an important role.

There is no record of a holding named Ashey in the Domesday Book, but Professor Koheritz in his book "Place names of the Isle of Wight", is of the opinion that Ashey was one of the estates which King Ethelred gave to the New Minster, Winchester, and seized by William the Conqueror and held by him under the name of Abedstone (the Abbot's Farm). Some historians however think that Ashey probably formed part of Kenistine (Knighton). Ashey must have been granted to the Abbey of Wherwell, near Andover some time after Domesday. Although the date of the grant is not known, the earliest reference to it is Pope Gregory IX's confirmation of 1228. The Abbey of Wherwell was founded about 980 AD, by Elfrida, the widow of King Edgar the Peaceable, in atonement for the crime of murdering her stepson Edward-the-Martyr in Corfe Castle.

In 1291, the manor was of considerable value with annual revenue of £41-6s-2d (£41.30). The boundaries of the manor, as far as can be ascertained were Rowlands Lane and the Binstead stream to the west; the seashore to the north; Smallbrook stream to the east; and Ashey Down to the south. The old manor house stood on the site of the present day East Ashey Farm. Although all traces of the house disappeared many years ago, we are told that it had large and elegant painted chambers with large and spacious rooms, also a chapel, burial ground and fish ponds. The fish ponds can still be seen today. The house was apparently still standing in 1624, as it is mentioned in a survey carried out in that year. The present house appears to have been built later in the century. The manor remained the property of the Abbey of Wherwell until the Dissolution but was leased by the last Abbess Morphita Kingsmill, to Giles Worsley and Elizabeth, his wife. The lease was dated 4 December 1538 and was for 50 years at a rental of £12 and ten couple of rabbits, and Giles Worsley was to pay the expenses of the steward and other officers of the Abbess when they held courts, which was twice a year.

The Abbey was a closed order, so a bailiff or steward was appointed to manage the manor, collecting rents due and holding court on behalf of the Lady of the Manor (the Abbess). The earliest steward known was Thomas who was in office by 1306, and was replaced about 1316 by Robert le Bonde. The manor was a "Liberty", which meant that it was outside the jurisdiction of the Sheriff and could hold Court Baron which dealt with estate matters, duties and receiving rents. This court was held in conjunction with a "View of Frankpledge" headed by the tithing man. He was responsible for the good behaviour of those living in the manor. Also held was Court Leet which handled the encroachments, nuisances, fraudulent weights, etc. The courts appointed the Parish constables each year to maintain law and order. Everyone aged 12 to 60 years who dwelt within the manor had to do suit to the court. Agnes Porter was brought before the courts in 1580 and was found guilty of witchcraft. According to the customs of the manor all her lands, goods and chattels were forfeited to the lord of the Manor.

According to the Poll Tax return of 1378 there were between 150 and 200 persons living within the manor boundaries. The northern boundary is interesting as it is defined as "Into the sea beyond low water as a man may reach the ground with an oar of 18 feet in length". Ryde was one of the three recognised ports (the others were Yarmouth and Shamford, near today's East Cowes). In about 1324 a watch house had been erected on the beach (Western Esplanade, today) and was manned by six soldiers. It would appear that they were of little use as the French burnt the village down in the latter part of the century. This raid resulted in a single gun being mounted on the bulwark which surrounded the Watch House. The Court Rolls give some details of goods supplied, such as 11lb of gunpowder in 1522. The bulwark was damaged several times by rough seas and had to be rebuilt at the expense of the manor.

In 1420 the Abbess had claimed the right to Ryde beach, which meant that all wreckage washed up including vessels wrecked in storms were hers to dispose of. The same year saw the Abbess claim the control of the boats taking people to and from Portsmouth and Ryde. Later in 1487 she appointed Richard Kene as Water Bailiff at a salary of 5s (25p) per annum. When the Abbey was closed by Henry VIII, the Abbess was granted a pension of £40 and the Sisters from £3-6s-8d to £6 each.

Giles Worsley continued as tenant and collector of dues until he was able to secure the grant of the manor by the Crown in 1544 for the sum of £759-19s-2d (£759.95p). Sir John Oglander said, "Giles was the first of the family to come to the Island from Lancashire" and was perhaps a younger brother of James who was nominated Captain of the Island in 1511 by Henry VIII. Giles died in 1558, leaving the manor to his son James, by his first wife. James died intestate at the age of 22 soon after his father and a claim was made for the estates by Sir Robert Worsley of Worsley, Lancashire; as a cousin and heir-at-law to Giles. This claim was contested by Richard Worsley, half brother of James, in the court of Wards and Liveries in 1563 and it was awarded that Sir Robert was to take a third, afterwards known as the manor of Ryde, while Richard was to have the part which had been bequeathed by Giles to his widow Margaret Worsley, comprising the site of the manor.

Thus Ryde was a parcel of Ashey and seems to have formed the portion which was awarded to Sir Robert Worsley by the courts in 1563, and in 1565 he sold it to Anthony Dillington. The track which connected Upper and Lower Ryde (today's St Thomas' Street) became very muddy in the winter and almost impassable. This resulted in the manorial court in 1574 ordering Mr Hobbs to construct a causeway for the inhabitants and a pack way for the horses. This gave a direct route (approx today's Union Street) between the two communities.

Upon Anthony Dillington's death in 1584 the estate passed to his son Robert, who was knighted in 1599. He died in 1608 and having no issue the estate passed to his nephew Robert who was created a Baronet in 1628. For this honour he paid £2,000. He died in 1656 and the estate passed to his eldest son Robert by his first wife. Upon his death in 1687 it passed first, to his eldest son Robert, and upon his death in 1689 to the second son John.

While the Dillington family were lords of the Manor there was little expansion, only some infilling in Upper Ryde. Drinking water was never plentiful in Ryde and the public wells had to be safeguarded. There were several wells in Upper Ryde, Tub Well, Nagg's Head, and the village green (today's St Thomas' Street). The court in 1526 ordered a fine of 10s (50p) to be levied on any person who abused the wells. Some tenants paid their dues to the manor in kind, such as a "dish of fresh sea bass" or "a cople (sic) of good fat capons". Other tenants gave their time to help the lord with his harvest. John Dillington sold the manor in September 1705 for £3,120 to Henry Player of Alverstoke, Hants (a brewer for the government). The new lord had a detailed survey carried out and a monetary value was placed on all holdings. This meant that all tenants had to pay their dues with cash. Henry Player was a businessman and did not wish to have fish and capons delivered to his door.

Shortly after his purchase Henry Player embanked the beach, built a house and a brewhouse. He also built two quays, the East Quay (or Ryde Quay) for the public to use and the West Quay for his private use. A toll was levied on goods landed and loaded. The money raised in the first two years was to be used to keep the quay in good repair and make a footway for the landing and embarking of foot passengers. By the 1720s it had to be repaired and a hardway had to be built some 700 feet x 6 feet out to the low water mark. An Admiralty chart dated 1783 shows the site of the causeway. The Watch House had fallen into decay and was leased to one Sweetman for 99 years. He had a house built on the site which later became the Black Horse Inn.

Henry Player started to hold his own manorial courts; in 1706 the Court Baron was presided over by the steward John Crouch. The custom of the manor stated that the lord of the Manor had to make a Bull, a Boar and a grinding stone available. Upon the death of Henry Player on 29 March 1711 the estate passed to his 5th son Thomas. This gentleman had St Thomas' Chapel built in 1719. This was the first place of worship in Ryde, which was part of the parish of Newchurch. The manor had to pay the Vicar of Newchurch £10 per year to officiate. The Chapel was consecrated on 27 June 1719 by the Bishop of Winchester. While Thomas Player was lord the village of Upper Ryde started to grow with more cottages built and an increase in the population. He died in 1721 and the manor passed to his only son William, who was an infant when he inherited. As an adult he worked at the navy office in London. Towards the end of the 18th century he purchased some farms which extended the manor to Binstead Stream. He also started to think about developing the estate.

In the last half of the 18th century sea bathing became popular with the wealthy classes. Doctors were recommending their patients to go to the seaside to swim and drink the sea water. William Player decided that the fields which separated the two communities could be used to build a number of new streets. He started to grant leases for building plots with land reserved for wide streets. These became Union Street, Melville Street, Nelson Street and Nelson Place. This gridiron pattern of streets brought the Upper and Lower Ryde together. William's decision was the start of Ryde becoming a seaside resort. By the mid 19th century it had grown into a town and had become one of the most fashionable watering places in England. It attracted minor Royalty, members of the Aristocracy, in fact anybody who had the means.

William died in 1792, but he had not made provision in his will for the continued growth of what was first called Middle Ryde. This meant that his widow Jane had to go to Parliament to obtain the Player Act which allowed her to set aside that section of William's Will dealing with his land. This released a wide area of building land. William had been the last lord of the Manor to own 95% of the land in central Ryde. He left the manor to his widow for her life time, then to his son George and daughter Elizabeth Lydia. George, having succeeded to half of the manor on his mother's death, decided to settle in Ryde. He took over Ryde Farm and had the fields landscaped. He also had Ryde House built about 1808. His sister Elizabeth Lydia was married in 1789 to John Lind of a Scottish family. He was the son of the famous James Lind who was known as "The Father of Nautical Medicine" and did much to rid the navy of scurvy. Both father and son worked at Hasler Hospital, Gosport. Elizabeth's half of the manor became the Lind Estate. John and Elizabeth had Westmont, Queens Road built in 1819 - 1821 as a family home.

During the first forty years of the 19th century Ryde saw many developments, for example local brewer John Cooper built in 1809 a jetty out to the low water mark. Its main use was for landing coal, etc but for one penny the public could also use it. In 1812 the Ryde Pier Act was passed and a new pier was constructed on the site of the old 18th century quay. It opened to the public in 1814 and John Cooper's landing stage was removed. Also in 1812 the first Free School was opened and was said to hold 340 children. The building still stands today (2007) in Melville Street. A second school for infants was built in Mount Street in 1830 and opened in the following year. Three years later a British School was built in St John's Road. Ryde did not officially become a town until 1829 but the word was used some years before.

The 18th century chapel of St Thomas had been at least twice enlarged but still worshippers had to stand outside the packed building. In 1827 George Player had the chapel taken down and replaced it with a much larger church designed by the London architect James Sanderson. At the same time the chapel of St James' was being erected. The Nonconformists started to hold services by 1799 and had their first chapel built in 1802 in Newport Street. This was followed by the Methodists who had a chapel erected in Spencer Road in 1811.

Residential properties were being built as fast as possible to meet demand. The Brigstocke Terrace was built 1826 - 1829 as a terrace of ten houses, a few years later St James' Terrace consisting of four houses. The first suburb Pelham Field was started from 1833 with development proceeding in Union Street and the surrounding streets. It was intended that Union Street would be lined with large detached houses but because of demand it very quickly changed to a street of high class shops.

The town had grown so rapidly that there was no adequate form of local government. Residents started to complain about the lack of services and in 1829 an Improvement Act was put before Parliament. This extract from preamble gives some idea of the conditions in the town "Whereas the Town of Ryde, in the Isle of Wight, in the County of Southampton, is become very populas and is much resorted to as a Watering Place and by persons passing and repassing to and fro from the Isle of Wight and whereas the said town is at present very ill paved and the streets, highways and other public passages therein are in many places very much out of repair, and the Police therein is very inefficient". With the passing of the Act, Town Commissioners were appointed to govern the Town and carry out improvements, such as providing paving, watching (Police), lighting and improving the streets. This led to the building in 1829 - 1831 of a Town Hall and market house in Lind Street to the designs of James Sanderson.

By the 1830s William Player's idea of a high class resort was coming into being and the streets he had planned were now full of buildings. The town could support a considerable number of trades, for example 15 bakers, 3 blacksmiths, 3 boat builders, 7 boot and shoe makers, 8 carpenters, 8 coal merchants and 5 straw hat makers. The population, which had been about 600 persons in 1795, had by 1831 reached 3,396 with 536 inhabited houses and was rising rapidly reaching 5,840 persons in 1841. James Courtney surveyed the town and produced a street map in 1836 which could be used today (2007) as a guide. From the 1840s through to the 1890s Ryde continued to expand and attract more people, with the population reaching 11,000 by the end of 1850s. It met the needs of the residents and tourists, more churches and schools were built, plus a hospital and the transport system was improved.

The Ryde that can be seen today (2007) shows that it was a Regency town expanded by the Victorians.

NOTE: The main source for the early history was Ashey Court Rolls and manorial documents held by the Isle of Wight Record Office.

CHAPTER 4

RYDE CHURCHES

St Thomas' Chapel early 19th century

St Thomas' Church

Ryde was once part of the large parish of Newchurch and villagers had to walk up to six miles to attend church. By the early years of the 1700s the population had grown to such an extent that in 1719 Thomas Player, lord of the Manor, had the first Chapel of St Thomas' built in Picket Close. The Right Rev Jonathan Trelawney, Bishop of Winchester, consecrated it on 27 June of that year. It was a Chapel of Ease to Newchurch, and endowed with a stipend of £10 payable yearly to the vicar of the parish to officiate in person or to send a deputy.

In the early 18th century, the population of Ryde was still expanding due to its growing popularity as a watering place, and it was decided to enlarge the chapel by adding another aisle parallel to the nave to accommodate the growing congregation. As this still did not provide adequate space, the chapel was demolished in 1826 and rebuilt on a larger scale in 1827 by George Player, grandson of the founder, at a cost of £3,500.

The Chapel designed by James Sanderson of Cork Street, London, who also designed Brigstocke Terrace, Ryde, was the same width as the old chapel but was much longer. In 1822 Elizabeth Lydia, younger daughter and co-heiress of George Player, married Captain Thomas Robert Brigstocke RN and ownership of the chapel eventually passed to them, remaining in their family's possession until 1957 when George Robert Brigstocke, the last in his line, passed away.

In the brief description of the rebuilt chapel found in the Historical and Commercial Directory of 1871, we learn the chapel was built in the Early English style of architecture, and consisted of a nave, chancel, north and south aisles with a tower and spire. The Church appears to have remained in its original form until 1947 when the spire, becoming unsafe, was taken down.

Services continued at the chapel until Sunday 28 June 1959, when doors closed for the last time. Sadly, the chapel fell into disrepair and the interior suffered occasional vandalism. Eventually the Church fell into such a sad and sorry state that in 1969 it was threatened with demolition.

In 1972, a group called The Friends of St Thomas' was formed with the aim of alerting the population of Ryde to the precarious state of one of its oldest buildings, in the hope they could eventually raise sufficient funds to restore the Church to its former glory. It still contains some fine memorials to the lords of the Manor and many other notable residents of Ryde.

In 1979, The Trust of St Thomas' was formed as a registered charity to take over the building on lease from the Portsmouth Diocese, and by applying for grants and donations it hoped to fund a complete restoration of the Church.

Events moved slowly, but in 1982, Medina Borough Council took over the churchyard and laid it out as a rest garden. Towards the end of 1985, the Trust was finally able to obtain a ten year lease on the building, and in January 1987, work started on the first stage of restoration. This entailed the repair of the roof, tower, west front, and windows on the south side.

The work was completed and the building transferred to the Isle of Wight Council. The hope it would once again become a central part of the community as a meeting hall, and exhibition and heritage centre has not happened yet.

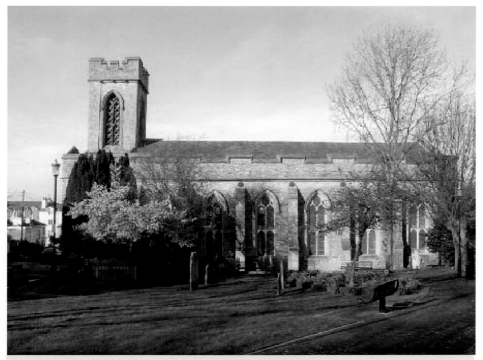

St Thomas' Church

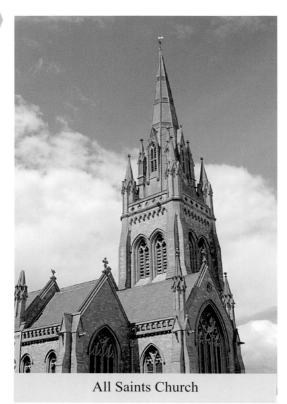
All Saints Church

All Saints Church dominates the skyline with its 186 feet steeple rising from a pinnacle tower. It is a fine example of a Victorian Decorated Gothic church. Designed by Sir Gilbert Scott, more famous for designing the Albert Memorial and St Pancras Station, London, it was built in three phases between 1869 and 1891.

HRH Princess Christian of Schleswig-Holstein laid the cornerstone in 1869 on behalf of her mother Queen Victoria. The nave, chancel and sanctuary were complete by 1872 when the Right Rev Samuel Wilberforce, Bishop of Winchester, and former Rector of Brighstone, consecrated the Church.

The architect's son, John Oldred Scott, designed the tower and spire added in 1881 and 1882. Finally, the cloister, crypt and octagonal vestry, designed by C Pemberton Leach who had a family connection with Ryde, were completed in 1891. The Church has a fine ring of eight bells cast by Messrs Taylor & Co in 1886.

In Ward Lock & Co's Guide of 1919, it states many authorities considered All Saints to be "the finest parish Church in the south of England". The nave has soaring arcades of six bays, the piers all having a different variety of foliage carved on the capitals with a similar design on the roof trusses.

Equally impressive is the beautiful alabaster and marble font standing at the west door, designed by Sir Gilbert Scott to commemorate the recovery from serious illness of the Prince of Wales (later Edward VII). The oak font cover, designed by an unknown local craftsman, is in memory of a parishioner, Mrs Harding.

There are two other significant designs of Gilbert Scott's in the Church. One is the pulpit of Derbyshire alabaster marble columns that won first prize in its class at the Great Exhibition of 1851. The figures arranged in pairs represent: St Peter and St Paul (apostles); Isaiah and Jeremiah (prophets); St John the Baptist and St Barnabas (preachers); St Stephen and St Alban (martyrs); the Virgin Mary and St Mary Magdalene and St Catherine and St Agnes.

The other example is in the Sanctuary. It is the altarpiece and reredos in alabaster and coloured marble behind the High Altar that depicts scenes from the Passion and Crucifixion. The altar table made from olive wood from the Holy land, dates from 1885. On the walls are fine murals designed by Clayton and Bell and, although they are now faded, they are still beautiful.

Most of the original stained glass was also by Clayton and Bell, but unfortunately, the Church lost much of this during World War Two. The best of the original glass is in the east window illustrating the "Te Deum". There is a beautiful window from 1913 of the Nativity by Ion Pace next to the north door. An example of modern stained glass is in the west window, replaced in 1951. It is by Lawrence Lee and depicts "Lord in Glory" and the "Saints' pilgrimage".

At the east end of the north aisle is the War Memorial Chapel consecrated in 1920 to the memory of those who died in World War One. It was erected at the same time as the Calvary, a representation of the passion and crucifixion of Christ, standing outside on the northeast corner looking down over the town. The Calvary now lists the names of those who lost their lives in the First and Second World Wars.

The Chapel of the Good Shepherd (formerly the vestry) stands at the end of the south aisle; it also has a beautiful reredos in alabaster and coloured marble designed by C Pemberton Leach. The four-light window over the altar depicts Psalm 23, "The Lord is my Shepherd".

The Church is very proud of its organ built by one of the greatest organ builders, "Father" Henry Willis in 1874. It was restored and electrified by his great-grandson Henry Willis IV in 1985; much of the original pipe work remains.

An interesting feature of the Church is the dignified North Porch erected to the memory of Prince Albert by members of the Royal Victoria Yacht Club. Over the centre is a niche containing a seated figure of Our Lord, his right hand raised in blessing. Figures of St John and St Andrew are in the other niches. All Saints has marvellous acoustics and is popular venue for visiting choirs and concerts.

Holy Trinity Church, Dover Street, Ryde

In 1839 when the Rev W Spencer Phillips BD was appointed vicar of the Parish of Newchurch, which included Ryde, he soon realised there was a need for a church in the town to serve the growing community.

The population had grown from 1,601 in 1811 to 5,840 in 1841. He quickly appointed a committee to raise funds for the project, and in two years, raised £5,806 by voluntary contribution and grants from various societies.

On 14 October Elizabeth Lind laid the first stone on a plot of land she and her family had kindly donated in Dover Street, Ryde. They had also generously given £1,500 to the building fund.

Designed by local architect Thomas Hellyer in the Early English Style, the Church provided seating for 800 people. 500 of the seats were set apart for free sittings forever; the remaining 300 were to be let to provide a yearly allowance for the incumbent. This was a common practice in those days.

When local builders Messrs Langdon and Denham had built up the Church to street level, the project unfortunately came to a halt due to legal difficulties.

The Honorable Lindsay Burrell, who was living in Ryde at the time, stood security for the cash required to continue, and another local builder, Thomas Dashwood, was employed to finish the project, including the tower and spire.

The Right Rev Charles Sumner DD, Bishop of Winchester, consecrated the Church on 28 October 1845, but it was still incomplete. There were no transepts and the spire was not finished until the following year when the Rev A J Wade MA, curate in charge, placed the final stone, the capstone, in position.

The Historical and Commercial Directory of 1871 notes, "the fine tower and spire affords an excellent landmark". It is hard to believe today that once Holy Trinity overlooked fields of grazing cattle. The London Gazette dated 26 May 1846, reported a district had been assigned to the new Church, and called The Chaplery District of the Holy Trinity, Ryde. The Church remained part of the Parish of Newchurch until 1863, when under the provision of the New Parishes Act of 1856, it became the Parish of Holy Trinity, Ryde. The incumbent Rev A J Wade MA, who served the Church from 1845 to 1893, became the first Vicar.

In 1848, the Church began to take on its cruciform plan when the south transept was erected at the expense of Rev Wade, with the north transept following some twelve years later providing extra seating.

A special organ chamber, designed by local architect, Francis Newman, was built in 1871 at a cost of £286. The organ remained there until 1927 when it was rebuilt and enlarged by Messrs Morgan and Smith, of Hove, Sussex, and re-erected at the east end of the north aisle.

The font by the west door is octagonal and of Caen stone with carving on its sides, and supported by short stone columns. It was given by the Yard Family. The inscription in Roman lettering around the bowl is by John Keeble, the famous priest and writer of many hymns. Keeble College, Oxford is named in his memory.

The South Chapel of St Martin contains the Parish memorial to those who fell in World War One. The reredos, unveiled in 1922 by Major-General John Edward Bernard Seeley, CB, CMG, DSO, Lord Lieutenant of Hampshire, show biblical heroes St Martin, St Michael the Archangel, St Christopher and St George. The stained glass above depicts the Martyrdom of St Alban and St Stephen, kneeling on cushions representing the Isle of Wight. Installed in 1966 through the generosity of the congregation, it was designed by Francis Skeat, of Harpenden, Hertfordshire.

The only surviving example of the glass that once filled the windows in this part of the Church is the trefoil high in the gable. The Church had a long association with the Jellicoe Family and the Union Jack in the Chapel was flown on HMS Iron Duke, flagship of the Admiral of the Fleet, Sir John (later

Earl) Jellicoe and presented by his sister, Edith Lucy Jellicoe.

Close by is an unusual bronze wall tablet featuring a submarine, a memorial to Lieutenant Commander Paul Eddis, commander of the submarine "L24" sunk during manoeuvres on 10 January 1924 off Portland, Dorset.

The brass ewer by the font was given in memory of Lieutenant Edmund Henry Jellicoe RN, who died in 1904. In the north aisle is a memorial tablet in memory of Elizabeth Davies (wife of Commander Arthur Davies RN and niece of Lord Nelson), erected by her children.

Inside Holy Trinity Church, Dover Street, Ryde

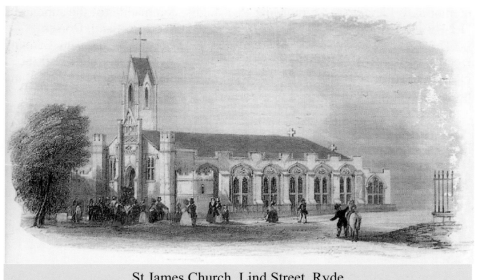

St James Church, Lind Street, Ryde

St James' Church in Lind Street, Ryde, a Proprietary Episcopal Chapel built in the Gothic style, first opened its doors for divine worship on 1 July 1827. The internal painting and decoration was not finished until the following spring.

The Church built by William Hughes Hughes Esq., Barrister at Law and at one time MP for Oxford, cost £6,000. The Church held 650 people including 200 free sittings, situated in the galleries, for the poor. The architect was Greenway Robins of Walworth, Surrey, and the first incumbent was the Rev Augustus Hewitt (brother to William Hughes Hughes).

The Church has had many ministers over the years, but one who stands out is the Rev Richard Waldo Sibthorp MA BD, who purchased the Church from its founder. He was the incumbent from 1830 to 1841, and during his time, St James' became well known for its evangelical preaching and high church ritual, attracting many notable families, who were holidaying in the town, to the services. One such family was that of the Duke of Buckingham from Buckingham Lodge, Ryde. In Peter Clarke's "From Ryde to Rome" he states, even "military and naval officers from Portsmouth would frequent the Church"

During his time as minister, Rev Sibthorp oversaw several alterations to the building. The organ placed in the western gallery was enlarged, and the flat ceiling over the nave moved to give the present open roof. Choir stalls were installed, and shields painted on the gallery beams.

In 1840 the Rev Thomas Jones, an 88 year old rector of Creaton, Northamptonshire, visited St James' and said in a letter it was "the very image of the beast" being fitted up in a very gaudy manner, like a theatre, and morning service lasted three hours with the organ taking up one hour of the three. Another person noted the organ played 33 times during the evening service. Rev Jones thought many attended for entertainment, and others to vent their sighs and sorrows. He did report the chapel was very full on Sundays and there was preaching in it nearly every day.

An article in the Hampshire Telegraph in January 1839, reported Rev Sibthorp, "should be praised for, despite the cold and rain during the winter months, people are attending his services two or three times a week to worship, even as early as 8 o'clock."

At that time the galleries were reserved for domestic staff of the many large houses in the area; menservants on one side and maids on the other.

Rev Richard Sibthorp had been one of the leading evangelicals but after close study of the Old Testament, he turned into a High Churchman transforming his church into a centre of ritualistic worship. In 1841 he left the church to become a Roman Catholic Priest.

After the upheaval caused by Rev Sibthorp's hasty departure had died down, Rev Augustus Hewitt, his predecessor, purchased the chapel and returned for his second incumbency. The church then reverted to the more traditional Evangelical doctrines.

In a rare book published in 1843, it states the Church is strictly proprietary and belongs to the officiating Minister. At the time, services were held at 10.30 am, 3.30 pm and 6.30 pm on Sundays, and at 7.00 pm on Thursdays. People who attended the Church had to pay with 'sittings' priced as follows:

- Middle aisle, in the body, per annum   £1- 4s- 0d
- Sides under the Galleries   £1-1s- 0d
- Front seats in the Gallery   15s- 0d
- Back seats in the Gallery   10s- 0d

There was also a proportion of Free Seats.

On 11 March 1903, during the incumbency of the Rev R R Cousens, an indenture conveyed the land and premises of the Church, dwelling house and vestry house to a group of Trustees – The Church Association and two local people, for the purposes of more effectively promoting Protestant and Evangelical doctrines. The present patron is The Church Society.

Another minister worthy of mention is the Rev Ernest Green, who served the Church for 40 years from 1934 to 1974, ably assisted by his wife. He served the Church during the difficult years of World War Two when some of the congregation were killed when a Portsmouth ferry, the Portsdown, struck a mine, and others died while on active service.

After the war, he initiated many important developments, the choir increased in size and special services were introduced such as, The Festival of Nine Lessons and Carols by Candlelight. The first of these took place in 1945 and they became an annual event.

In contrast to the opinions of Rev Jones in 1840, when Sir John Betjeman visited Ryde in 1954, and particularly asked to see the Chapel, he exclaimed, "There's a wonderful period piece for you".

During Rev Green's incumbency, extensive improvements were made to St James' with a special appeal launched in 1968 to fund the alterations.

The Church hall was the first area to be renovated. Warm air heating was installed, a kitchen, committee room and cloakrooms were constructed and repairs to the roof and windows carried out. Work then started on the Church at a cost of approximately £16,000. The roof was renewed, and alterations made to the west front that is now adorned with a giant fish (the secret sign of early Christians).

Alterations inside the Church included warm air heating, a new choir vestry, a foyer for the bookstall, the nave shortened with a screen allowing passers-by to look into the Church, and the interior was completely redecorated. The architect for the project was Mr R P Thomas DFC of Portsmouth and it cost almost £22,000, much of which was raised at The Church Shop, High Street and by generous donations. In December 1969, a service of thanksgiving for the restoration of the Church was held at which the Bishop of Portsmouth preached.

Unfortunately, early in 1972, Rev Green's health started to deteriorate giving cause for concern, and in July of the same year, his wife suffered a fatal stroke. At her funeral service many people paid tribute to her devotion and dedication to the church. Rev Green rallied for a while and preached to a full Church for the last time at the 1973 Carols by Candlelight Service. He passed away in March 1974.

St John the Baptist Church

St John the Baptist Church, Oakfield, Ryde, was consecrated on 18 July 1843 by the Bishop of Winchester to serve as a district chapel for the Parish of St Helens. It was built by Charles Langdon & Co. on land donated by Sir John Simeon, Bart of Swainston House, Calbourne, and owner of St John's House, Appley, opposite the site.

Local architect Thomas Hellyer produced the first plans in 1841. The cost of the building totalled £1630-19s-2d and was raised by donations and private subscription. The original Church was considerably smaller than today's. Cruciform in design, it consisted of a small nave, short north and south transepts and a small chancel; there were no side aisles or Lady Chapel.

The Church was built to serve the small village of Oakfield and the many agricultural workers living in the area at the time. As the population of Ryde grew and the residential area spread from the seafront up to St John's, it became clear the Church needed to be enlarged and plans were drawn up to provide additional space.

First, a side aisle was built on the south side of the nave, with a gallery over the west end reached by a small semi-spiral stairway housed in a specially built turret in the west wall. This additional space provided seating for 160. An organ (15 stops) was built in the gallery and where the Lady Chapel is now situated, a vestry was built.

The congregation continued to increase in the mid-1860s and further extensions were planned. A north aisle was built to match the south aisle, and a new font placed at the west end.

With additional seating in the north aisle and other extensions, the gallery was removed and the organ rebuilt in an organ chamber. The problem of accessing the new side aisles was overcome by building a row of graceful arcades on each side of the nave whose stone pillars and pointed arches formed the support for the roof. The lighting in the Church was improved by the addition of more windows on each side of the nave roof, and in the walls of the side aisles, all containing attractive Victorian stained glass.

The consecration of the enlarged Church took place on 3 December 1870, and the new Parish of St John the Baptist, Oakfield, declared. The chancel was extended again in 1954 and the east window dismantled. The window was replaced and reglazed with the sections of stained glass reassembled piece by piece.

The Lady Chapel or south chapel was erected in memory of Lord Calthorpe who lived nearby at Woodlands Vale, and the stained glass windows and wall tablets are all memorials to members of the Calthorpe Family. The heavy brass cross and candlesticks on the High Altar were given in memory of General Sir Samuel Browne of the Indian Army, remembered for inventing the Sam Browne belt. He lived in St John's Park, Ryde, and died in 1901.

The octagonal stone font, dating from 1893, stands at the west end of the Church, behind which is a batik screen depicting the Baptism of Christ and scenes of families and children worldwide made by Irene Ogden. Mother Teresa, depicted in one corner of the screen, is tending the poor and sick children of Calcutta, India. At the west end of the south aisle is the Children's Library, previously known as Children's Corner. Established in 1912 by the Rev Henry William Pearce with the help of his wife, it is area of the Church where children can gather together to find their own way of expressing ideas and thoughts.

In the years 1979 – 1980, during the incumbency of the Rev Edward Fox, a significant change was made in the pattern of worship at St John's. The pulpit was moved from its traditional position and a new nave altar erected on a dais in a more central position, so the Holy Eucharist could be presented from the midst of the congregation. The altar is covered in a cloth of a coloured design suitable for all seasons of the liturgical year made by the Sisters of St Cecilia's Abbey, Appley.

St John the Baptist Church, Oakfield, Ryde

St Michael and All Angels Church

St Michaels and All Angels Church, Swanmore, Ryde

The Parish Church of Swanmore, St Michael and All Angels, was built in 1857 in the Medieval French style and consecrated by the Bishop of Winchester in 1863. The Church is cruciform in shape. The central square tower is nearly 90 feet high with three bells hung on the second level. It commands panoramic views across the Solent from the top.

The interior is mainly sandy-coloured brickwork with coloured patterns of red, black and grey bricks together representing the four elements, earth, air, fire and water.

On the north side of the transept is St George's Chapel, containing the organ and war memorial. The Lady Chapel is on the south side. Its painted ceiling is by Arthur Moore and depicts the nine orders of angels.

The Sanctuary has a high vaulted roof and seven windows with marble shafts. The Chancel screen has twelve arches between polished marble pillars and the twelve apostles stand in the trefoiled niches. The integrated pulpit features Moses, Elijah, St John the Baptist, St Mark, St Luke, St Paul and St Barnabas.

The crucifixion window shows the hands of the Father over the Cross but the memorial stained glass in four other windows was lost during World War Two.

The High Altar, a centenary gift from the congregation in 1963, is a stone table supported by large stone crosses. The statue of St Michael was a gift in 1970. There are also stone statues of Our Lady and Child given by the Sunday School in 1926 and of St Joseph and St Anne.

Two lancets in the west wall have stained glass depicting St Raphael and St Michael by Lavers and Westlake.

The first vicar, the Rev Richard Wix, was a significant figure, not only in the parish but also, nationally within the Anglican Church. He was part of The Oxford Movement, and fought for the right to burn candles at the altar and incense during services, both illegal practices in the day that could result in the suspension or even imprisonment of the clergy.

Rev Wix defied his Bishop's orders and his curates were refused licences to officiate at services. He was called to The Court of Arches in London to explain his actions and was heavily fined but still continued the practice.

Within a year, a more moderate Bishop, Samuel Wilberforce, former rector of Brighstone, was appointed and the assistant curates were licensed.

A brass tablet in the Church featuring a bishop is a memorial to Samuel Wilberforce who later became Bishop of Oxford.

Inside St Mary's Roman Catholic Church

St Mary's Roman Catholic Church in High Street, Ryde, was built at the sole expense of The Right Honourable Elizabeth Julia Georgina, Countess of Clare. She had moved to Ryde to be near her brother, The Honourable Lindsay Burrell, a keen sailor and a founder member of the Royal Victoria Yacht Club, after separating from her husband, John Fitzgibbon, 2nd Earl of Clare.

Once established in Ryde she began to attend services at the Anglican Church of St James' in Lind Street, where the Rev Richard Waldo Sibthorp MA was incumbent. Here she was to witness a church service far different to those she had attended before, as Rev Sibthorp's services, which had already started to cause concern to the members of The Protestant Society in the town, gradually became a mixture of Roman Catholic and Anglican doctrines. He eventually left St James' in 1841 to become a Roman Catholic.

The Countess was very interested in the Catholic faith as she searched for a belief she felt was more in keeping with the teachings of the early Fathers of the Church. With her companion Charlotte Elliot, she travelled to Europe to visit the churches and cathedrals of Catholic Europe to learn more.

She was stunned by the beautiful and imposing cathedrals she visited on her journey, and when she finally reached Rome, she was thrilled to be in the Eternal City with its stunning art and architecture.

It was here she met Thomas Grant, who was later to become the Bishop of Southwark, from The English College, who gave her instruction in the Catholic Faith. He later introduced her to Father William Hunt who became the Provost of Westminster, and he received her into the Catholic Church in St Peter's Basilica, Rome, on 7 September 1841.

When she returned to Ryde, the Countess attended Mass at St Thomas of Canterbury Church in Newport. She realised there was a need for a church in Ryde as not everyone could travel the seven miles to Newport in a pony chaise as she could; others had to walk.

At first, the small Roman Catholic community in the town attended Mass at a small villa in Goldsworth Grove (between West Street and Victoria Street) conducted by the recently ordained Father Thomas Richardson. The Countess wanted to build a fine church to reflect the importance of her conversion, and when a plot of land in the High Street came up for auction she was determined to acquire it.

A gardener, Mr Mayne, was asked to bid for the plot on her behalf, as there was still a lot of unrest among The Protestant Society in the town due to the "Sibthorp affair". The Countess engaged Joseph Aloysius Hansom, of Hansom Cab fame, as architect. Initially he wanted to design a Classical style church but on seeing the High Street plot, he decided an Early English Gothic design was more in keeping with the surroundings.

Once Bishop Griffiths of the London District, and the relevant officials in Rome had accepted the plans, Thomas Dashwood, a local builder was employed to carry out the project.

The foundation stone was laid by Father John Clark of Gosport, (representing Bishop Griffiths), together with Father Thomas Fryer of Newport, and Father Thomas Richardson of Ryde, on the third Sunday of

Advent, 17 December 1844. The Church opened 18 months later. It is built in local ragstone with Caen stone dressing on the west front and had a tomb-shaped High Altar, a replica of the one in York Minster but this was removed in the 1960s.

The first Low Mass was said on Trinity Sunday, 7 June 1846 before all the building works were completed. Father William Hunt who had baptised the Countess into the Catholic faith in Rome conducted the service in the south aisle (now the Lady Chapel). Newly appointed rector, Father John Telford, had advised this Mass should be a quiet affair because of the continued hostility towards Catholics, and the recent death of Pope Gregory XVI.

Later in the year, when the internal furnishings of the Church were completed, Father John Clark of Gosport celebrated a High Mass on 22 September with Father John Telford and Father William Hunt. The Countess would hear Mass in her own private chapel situated above the sacristy. The first Episcopal visit took place on 27 June 1847, when Bishop Thomas Griffiths confirmed 92 people.

Monsignor Thomas Grant, the first Bishop of Southwark, consecrated the Church to the glory of God and in honour of the "Immaculate Heart of Mary for the conversion of sinners" on 21 May 1863. The Church has beautiful stained glass windows that were added between 1860 and 1880. The Lady Chapel and Shrine of Our Lady in the southeast corner were built in 1893. The shrine has an altar designed by Augustus Welby Pugin with a carving of Our Lady of Walsingham and beautiful murals of various decades of the rosary.

In the 1850s the Countess's generosity also provided St. Mary's School, (now the parish hall), paid the salary of two teachers and built a row of cottages in St Mary's Passage for church workers.

St Mary's Roman Catholic Church Plaque

Congregational Church

The Congregational Church stood at the corner of George Street and Melville Street and had a long and interesting history dating back to 1799. Through the Church Minute Book of 1816, held at the Isle of Wight Record Office, Newport, we are able to gain an insight into its history.

A gentleman from London, Robert Curling, was visiting Ryde in 1799 and noted with regret there was nowhere for the poor to receive religious instruction. Together with the help of some friends, he set about finding a solution. They soon hired a barn and engaged a young man as a teacher to instruct the children. Before long over 100 children attended and were taught to read using stories from the Bible.

On Sunday, religious instruction was given to the children, their parents, and any others who wished to attend. Eventually the barn became too small, and in 1802 a chapel was built on the roadside above Upper Ryde, (now Newport Street), funded once again by Mr Curling and his friends.

For several years, the Church was without its own pastor, but neighbouring ministers kindly held services during the week and on Sunday, a minister would come from The Church Academy at Gosport to conduct services.

As attendance at the Church continued to grow, another larger Church was planned, on land in George Street donated by James Kirkpatrick. With donations, subscriptions and the sale of the old chapel, the project went ahead.

James Kirkpatrick with the Rev A Douglas of Reading, Berkshire, officiating, laid the foundation stone and on 20 November 1816, the Church opened for public worship with seating for nearly 350 people. Still with no settled pastor of their own, the Rev T S Guyer, who had often taken services, was approached. He agreed, and on 26 November 1817, he was ordained.

The Church continued to be enlarged to accommodate the ever-growing congregation and on 2 September 1837, the first marriage took place between Henry Wicker and Margaret Jennings. A smaller chapel, costing £132-6s, was opened in Green Lane, Ashey, in 1839 with money raised through subscriptions, and another followed at Langbridge in 1846; the same year in which the long serving Rev Guyer died.

During 1854, while the Rev R Ferguson was minister, plans were made to erect a new chapel on the site, and although he left shortly after, he made a generous donation to start the fund.

The new chapel was erected at a cost of £2,500, and in White's Directory of 1859, it is described as handsome in the Italian style with approximately 850 sittings.

Built like a Roman temple, it was lit from the roof, as there were no side windows. The Church was very ornamental with Corinthian pilasters and a handsome portico with four pillars supporting a pediment crowned by a small but elegant cupola.

In 1859, the Rev Cultart came to the Church and, under his guidance and leadership, the Church continued to flourish. Attendance increased and the chapels built at Green Lane and Langbridge became free of debt.

In 1866, the Church celebrated its Jubilee, but unfortunately, a few years later on 29 April 1870 the Church was destroyed by fire. By the November of that year, John Kemp Welsh had laid the foundation stone for a new Church.

The inscription read:

"Congregational Church
First built AD 1816
The Rev T S Guyer, minister
Taken down and rebuilt 1855
The Rev R Ferguson, minister
Destroyed by fire 29th April 1870"

The Historical and Commercial Directory of 1871 gives a brief description of the new Church nearing completion - Designed by Richard J Jones, it was to be built in 14th century style, modified to suit Protestant Nonconformists of the 19th century.

Built of Swanage stone with Bath stone dressing, the plan consisted of a nave with seven bays separated from the north and south aisles by arcades of iron columns carrying wooden arches with ornamental tracery in the spendrils. The roof was to be high pitched and eventually covered with tiles. There were to be galleries around three sides of the building and at the east end, a space reserved for the organ. There was also to be a raised platform for the choir with the pulpit in front.

The new Church opened in 1872 with the Rev Theodore Hooke as its minister.

Over the years, the congregation grew smaller and smaller and was unable to maintain the upkeep of the Church. They bought a house in Upton Road and built a chapel in the grounds. The Church in George Street closed in 1974 and was taken down. Richwoods Furniture Store stands on the site today.

Ryde Baptist Church, George Street

Prior to 1847 the few Baptists in Ryde worshipped with the Congregationalists, but they had a desire to have their own place of worship and in the summer of 1847 a room was hired in George Street where services were conducted by local preachers.

In November 1848 an upper room in a house in the Colonnade, Lind Street, Ryde, was licensed and opened for Divine Worship.

Ryde Baptist Church was officially formed in January 1849 and on that date Mary Pidder presented an ordinance service consisting of a chalice and salver with collecting plate to the Church. The minister, the Rev William Newell was not officially appointed until October of that year.

The Rev J H Saunders succeeded Rev Newell from December 1850 until April 1851. In January 1851 a new building in John Street, ultimately intended as a School Room opened as the temporary chapel.

After Rev Saunders, the Rev D R Watson took over from December 1851 until the end of 1854. He appears to have been a somewhat difficult man and not easy to get on with and after he left the Church was in a chaotic state. A series of resolutions were passed that were intended to restore harmony and certain members who had been expelled were asked to return.

During the year 1855, the Revs James Harrison and E W Davies held the pastorate, each serving for a few months only.

In November 1855, the Rev Samuel Cox of Southsea, Hampshire, accepted an invitation to become the Minister and Pastor of the Church. He served for three years, resigning in May 1858. During that period, he gathered many new members and the Sunday School commenced in February 1856 with Mr C Colenutt as its first superintendent. Rev Cox later became widely known and honoured as one of the country's finest scholars. He wrote and edited many books and contributed to The Nonconformist, The Freeman, The Christian Spectator and The Quiver. His best known work Salvator Mundi was published in 1887. St Andrew's University awarded him the degree of Doctor of Divinity in 1882, the same degree was also offered to him by Edinburgh and Aberdeen.

In November 1859, the Rev J B Little was invited to the Church at John Street and he commenced his ministry there in January 1860. In the summer of 1861, it was resolved to build a chapel on ground in George Street. For some months, the chapel in John Street had proved too small to accommodate the congregation, and the evening service was held in the Victoria Rooms, Lind Street. This was inconvenient and an application was made and granted for the use of the Town Hall during the erection of the new chapel. In March 1862 Sir I Morton Peto, Bart, MP, laid the first stone of the new chapel that was completed and opened on 9 October of the same year.

Rev Little resigned in August 1864 and was succeeded by the Rev Thomas Astor Binns in October 1864. There must have been some dispute about the appointment of Rev Binns as in March 1865 there was a resolution declaring the "Dissolution of the Membership". After continuing in a state of suspended animation for a year, the Church was reconstituted with forty nine members in March 1866, with Rev Binns still the minister.

Some of those formerly connected with the Church were dissatisfied; they highly disapproved of Rev Binns wearing a gown in the pulpit. This and other matters resulted in the formation of a second Baptist Church that was also publicly recognised in March 1866. This Church assembled for some time in a room in the High Street, later it moved to a building at the bottom of Park Road, Ryde, and continued to exist until 1912.

The George Street Church seems to have enjoyed some prosperity, by 1866 all the building debt was cleared, and the Sunday School was successful with over 150 scholars.

In April 1874, Rev Binns announced he intended to resign and move abroad. The congregation received the news with deep regret and he was asked to stay on until a suitable successor could be found.

In April 1875, the Rev J R Chamberlain of Bath accepted an invitation to become pastor of the Church. His ministry was not particularly eventful and he resigned in January 1880, entered the Congregational ministry and moved to Brading Congregational Church where he remained until his death.

The Rev Harry Collings served as minister for a very brief time and he was followed by the Rev William Steadman Davis from Trinity Church, Huntingdon, in June 1881. Rev Davis served the Church for six years, the Monthly Missionary Prayer Meeting was introduced during his time and there was a marked development in the musical side of Sunday services. A choir was formed and a fund was opened to purchase an organ, which was installed by January 1885. His resignation in December 1887 was met with sadness.

For the next twenty years from 1888 to 1907, the Church came under the ministry of the Rev Edward Bruce Pearson and under his guidance it thrived and the congregation grew. A marked feature of his ministry was the frequent Days or Weeks of Prayer, a Young Christians' Band was formed and a Benevolent Society and there were all kinds of development in the organisation and activities of the Church. Rev Pearson was a greatly loved man of noble spirit and was described as 'a great peace-maker'. He resigned from the ministry in September 1907 and he died in May 1920.

In July 1908, the Rev H H Turner commenced his ministry; he was an active aggressive evangelist who plunged into the work by organising a "Gospel Forward Movement" for social development. It included a Benevolent Fund, a Coal Club, a Cycling Club and the publication of the Monthly Messenger.

The Movement covered a broad area and the Church services were given an evangelistic note, the constitution of the Church was revised with a new set of rules and some alterations were made to the pulpit and the choir stalls. During this pastorate, a church magazine, The Baptist Record, commenced.

Rev Turner resigned in October 1913 to take up work in Newport and the following September the Rev J E Compton became the minister. This new minister took steps to modernise the Church and the services. The introduction of individual cups for the Communion Service was readily adopted but the introduction of a new Hymn book and the requirement to sing 'Amen' at the end of hymns was met with much resistance for a short time.

Rev Compton resigned in July 1918, which led to the coming of the Rev M Lister Gaunt in March 1919. During his ministry, electric lighting was installed in the chapel in 1919 and a Manse in Vernon Square was purchased in 1920. Membership of the Church rose to 186 in 1923. In 1925, the original tower, considered unsafe, was replaced with a shortened one.

Following Rev Gaunt's resignation in 1930, the Rev Herbert G Drake entered the pastorate in August 1931 and served for five and half years. During this period, 77 members joined the Church.

In 1932 a well planned and beautifully executed scheme of internal decoration was carried out and during 1935 a new heating apparatus was installed at a cost of £56-10s-0d. Rev Drake left in March 1937 and Rev Gaunt stepped in again until the coming of the Rev P Franklin Chambers in June 1938.

Two important events mark the early days of Rev Chambers' ministry – the purchase of Grantham House, Monkton Street, to become known as Christ Church Manse, and installation of the Hammond Electric Organ.

The dark years of World War Two forced limitations on the work of the church, but with the leadership and charm of Rev Chambers the fellowship was maintained and prospered. During 1940 Fortiphone Aids for the Deaf were installed in a number of pews, these were the gift of Mrs Thorne in memory of her husband.

In 1941, the house next to the Manse was blitzed causing severe damage but no one was injured.

Rev Chambers retired in February 1944 and in May of that year the Rev W M Tristram was invited to the pastorate. His ministry lasted only two years but he was considered a true friend of the people and was held in high esteem and affection in the town.

The Rev E J Willis took over the ministry in June 1947 until 1952 when he left Ryde and was replaced by the Rev Walter Fancutt.

During the late 1940s and the 1950s, the Church continued to grow and as well as Sunday services and the Sunday School there were many meetings such as Boys Brigade, Girls Brigade, Bible classes, etc. during the week. In addition, there were church outings, picnics, garden parties and the like.

In the early 1950s, decisions were made to sing the Lord's Prayer and not to sing Amen at the end of hymns. The name plates were removed from the pews and a notice put up saying all pews were free. Previously some places in the chapel had been purchased to help raise funds for the Church.

The Hammond organ was in such a bad condition, caused by wood beetle infestation, the decision was taken to destroy it. Ten years later it was replaced, but by an organ in a similar condition.

In 1957, discussions on the renovation of the Church began. Also in 1957 Rev Fancutt left and was replaced by the Rev Hugh Wrigley in May 1958. By 1960, membership of the Church was 117 but church meetings were often only attended by 17 or so people. In the early 1960s, the Church supported the Billy Graham Relays and there was a Bible Study Group, however this was a time of decline for the Church.

In 1962, a row over Freemasonry broke out and the Treasurer and Secretary, both Freemasons, resigned and the Church was left without officers for a time. The matter was eventually resolved amicably, the minister left and by 1965 the Secretary and Treasurer had resumed their earlier roles.

Rev Wrigley was replaced by the Rev A J Symonds, until his death in July 1966 when the Rev I Jones took over. He supported more programmes of evangelism and there were growing activities with other churches. In 1969, a beat group called The Relayers proposed to start a coffee bar and the Church gave what encouragement it could. By 1969, woodworm was creeping into the Church through the organ sound box causing noticeable deterioration in the building and there were problems with vandalism.

Church membership remained at around 100 but by the early 1970s, the church was active but not growing. Rev Jones retired in 1974 to be succeeded by the Rev J Taylor and then by the Rev Gerald Clarke.

In 1987, approaches were made to the Church involving relocating the Church; this scheme eventually fell through. In June 1995, a fire, caused by an electrical fault, started near the entrance and the interior and roof were badly damaged. The Church was soon able to meet in the room at the back but they lost members and a drop in income meant there was not enough money to support a pastor and morale was low. Redevelopment was again considered but there were setbacks. Somerfield approached the Church, offering to provide a new site in George Street where The Foyer project is now. This plan fell through when Somerfield were able to obtain the car parking they needed without purchasing the Church.

The Church survived many difficulties and the Rev Richard Steel postponed his retirement to be its part-time, transitional minister. A plan put forward for rebuilding the Church involved adding an extra floor and the concept of a community centre for the local people downstairs. The scheme was strongly supported by the Baptist Union and obtained a Regeneration Grant for the creation of the community centre. In January 2003, with Home Mission support, the Rev Jane Kingsnorth was appointed as full-time minister. Six months later the building work started.

In August 2004, the new George Street Centre, home of The Ryde Baptist Church, opened. In spite of the heat from the fire, the stained glass window behind the worship area remained intact and was put back in position.

The new centre continues to thrive under Rev Jane Kingsnorth and hosts a number of community events and clubs throughout the week as well as the church services and a café on the ground floor.

Ryde Social Heritage Group held an evening meeting for the launch of its new website, www.rshg.org.uk, in the George Street Centre in March 2006. RSHG continues to hold Quarterly Members' Meetings at the centre.

Rev Alexander Frederick De Gex, JP
1860 – 06/04/1931

He was assistant priest of St Michael and All Angels Church, Swanmore, Ryde, for nearly three years until ill health forced him to resign the position shortly before his death in 1931.

He was previously curate of Holy Trinity Church, Ryde, for the four years from 1924. In all, Rev de Gex spent 49 years in the ministry.

Educated at Wells College, he was ordained in 1882, was curate of St John's Church, Bridgwater, Somerset, until 1886, and held a similar position at Lower Brixham, Devon, between 1885 and 1886. From then until 1901 he was rector at Angersleigh, Somerset, rural dean at South Molton, Devon, from 1910 to 1916, and rector at Meshaw, Devon, from 1891 to 1924.

In 1924, he became a Fellow and Subwarden of St Michael's College, Tenbury, Worcestershire, founded by Sir Frederick Gore Ouseley, the famous composer.

Rev de Gex preached in different parts of the country for The National Society. In 1904, he was made a Justice of the Peace for the county of Devon.

He died on Monday 6 April 1931 at his home 16 Monkton Street, Ryde, after being taken seriously ill a few weeks before Christmas 1930.

Henry Brent
25/05/1848 – 29/04/1923

Son of the Rev Daniel Brent, Vicar of Grendon, Northants, he was an engineer in the locomotive department of the Isle of Wight Railway for many years. Henry was also churchwarden, sidesman and superintendent of the Boys' Department of St John's Church Sunday School.

He died on 29 April 1923 at Lynmouth, High Park, Ryde, where he lived with his sister Florence Ellen Brent.

Charles Bernard Hair
1873 – 1940

He was the organist and choirmaster at St Michael and All Angels Church, Ryde, for over 40 years. Charles Hair became an expert in Gregorian Music and introduced many people to the beauty of this kind of music.

The choirboys were his pride and joy. Many 'Old Boys' of the Church can trace their love of music to his devotion and reverence for the faith in the lessons he taught and the inspiration he brought to them.

He struggled with semi-blindness, pain and weakness to give service to the Church and played his last service, the Hallelujah Chorus, at evensong on Easter Day 1940.

Charles Bernard Hair died on 3 April 1940. Many local musicians, choristers and his pupils attended his funeral. He lived in Green Street, Ryde.

Father John Telford
Rector of St Mary's Church, Ryde, 1845 - 1865

Born on 26 January 1814, John Telford was ordained in 1838 by Bishop Thomas Griffiths, and appointed Chaplain at St Georges-in-the-Fields, London, in August 1840.

He became friends with the famous Victorian Gothic Architect, Augustus Welby Pugin who was working on St George's Church. He assisted in laying the foundation stone of the new Southwark Cathedral, London, on 26 May 1841.

In December 1845, he came to Ryde, swapping places with Father Richardson, the first minister at Ryde, as Rector of the new St Mary's Church.

John Telford died on 7 November 1865. Bishop Grant of Southwark presided at the funeral. After the Requiem Mass, hundreds followed the coffin in procession along the High Street and Hill Street to Ryde Cemetery. The Isle of Wight Times gave a very favourable report, unusual in this period, saying they admired his Christian principles and warm friendly nature although they profoundly disagreed with his religion.

There is a brass commemorative plaque in the Sanctuary of St Mary's Church in memory of his work in Ryde.

Monsignor John Cahill
2nd Bishop of Portsmouth 1841 - 1910

John Cahill was born on 2 September 1841, the son of Thomas and Joanne Cahill.

He went to Old Hall Seminary and was ordained at Bermondsey by Bishop Grant of Southwark on 4 October 1864.

Thomas and Edward, his two older brothers, also became priests.

His first appointment was at Portsea, Hampshire, before coming to Ryde in 1866 as Curate. Two years later, he became Rector, succeeding Father Stephen Phillips. He was known for his like of the ritual and ceremony of Catholic worship and for rendering powerful sermons.

In 1882, he was appointed the Vicar General of the Portsmouth Diocese and in 1883, persuaded the Sisters of Mercy, Abingdon, to open a boarding school in the Convent on the north side of St Mary's Church.

In 1887 he was created a Domestic Prelate, and in 1892 Protonotary Apostolic. In May 1900, he was ordained Titular Bishop of Thagara by Bishop Bourne and left Ryde for Portsmouth in August to succeed Bishop Vertue.

Lieutenant Colonel Hamilton and Mrs Randolph, two of the oldest members of the parish, presented him with an Episcopal ring, gold cross and chain, a mitre and Roman missal on behalf of the congregation of St Mary's.

He frequently returned to Ryde and welcomed the Benedictine monks at their temporary home at Appuldurcombe where he blessed the Holy Oils each year at the invitation of the Abbot, Dom Paul Delatte. He was pleased when they bought the Quarr Abbey ruins in 1907, as another religious community would reside in his beloved Ryde.

He died on 2 August 1910 and is buried in Ryde Cemetery near his two brother priests. His coffin was brought back to Ryde by special paddle steamer after the funeral service in Portsmouth accompanied by the clergy and choir who sang psalms and litanies on the journey.

CHAPTER 5

EDUCATION IN RYDE

Introduction

The first schools in England accessible to the mass population were established by the churches to teach religious studies. In 1811, The National Society was set up by the Anglican Church and in 1814 The British and Foreign Society was established. Both set up schools designed to provide basic elementary education as well as religious studies for as many children as possible. They became known as the National and British Schools respectively.

St Thomas' National School

The first school in Ryde, St Thomas' National School, was founded in Melville Street in 1812. The Countess Spencer was responsible for raising the funds to build the school and she persuaded the lady of the Manor to give a piece of land with a peppercorn rent.

At the time, the area would have been fields on the edge of town. The building, later known as the Vectis Hall, can be seen on the 1819 map of Ryde and was originally two large rooms with classrooms attached and could take up to 340 boys and girls.

The school moved to new buildings in Green Street in 1857 and there has been a school on the site ever since, today called Greenmount Primary School.

In 1862 under a revised Code of Regulations, head teachers were required to keep log books and make regular entries, at least once a week recording staff, school progress and events affecting life in the school and neighbourhood. In practice, the level of information varied considerably according to the preferences of the head teacher with some making daily entries and others handing the job to pupil teachers.

These log books, where they still exist, are a valuable source of information on the school, the staff and pupils, the local area, local and national events, illness and death and the behaviour of pupils. They are the principal source, together with any surviving Minute Books, for researching the social history of the school and its area.

Ryde Social Heritage Group was able to participate in Greenmount Primary School's 150th anniversary celebrations and presented the school with a selection of transcribed school log books from the 1860s to 1916. Two committee members were invited to attend the celebration day on 13 July 2007 where the children displayed their work on the history of their school and performed a special dance interpretation of 150 years of the school.

Excerpts from Green Street National School log reveal much information:

- 9 September 1862, one child taken away because made to do school needlework.
- 22 September 1862, attendance smaller than usual on account of a social tea gathering of dissenters.
- 28 November 1862, half holiday in consequence of the Consecration of a Cemetery by the Bishop of Winchester.
- 9 September 1863, a great many girls absent on account of sickness at home. Scarlet Fever and Diphtheria prevalent.
- 4 May 1864, distributed a number of tickets to the children to admit them to a public entertainment at the Victoria Rooms in Lind Street.
- 15 June 1864, Smallpox becoming very prevalent in the neighbourhood, several children sick and others absent on that account.

Later school admission and attendance registers were introduced to record the names of pupils, details of their parents or guardians, their previous schools, where applicable, and a daily record of attendance in the school.

The 1870 Education Act, drafted by William E Forster, a Liberal MP and Vice-President of the Committee of Council on Education, divided the country into about 2,500 school districts.

School Boards were elected by the ratepayers in each district. Their role was to examine the existing provision of elementary education in their district and if there were not enough school places, to build and maintain schools out of the rates. They were to provide elementary education for all children aged between 5 and 12 and could make their own by-laws allowing them to set fees or admit children of poorer families for free.

Education became compulsory in 1880 and free to all in 1891. It was not until 1902, when the Balfour Education Act was passed, funding was provided for secondary schools.

Ryde School Board

The Board was formed in 1871 and set fees and holidays for the schools.
Fees:

- Under 7 years of age 2d per week
- Above seven years of age 3d per week
- More than one child in the family, 2d each child per week

An additional 1d was charged for extra subjects at the school's discretion.

Holidays:
- 1 week at Easter
- 3 weeks summer, commencing the 1st Monday in August
- 2 weeks at Christmas

St John's Road School

In June 1871, the trustees and subscribers of the Ryde British Schools, established in St John's Road, Ryde, in 1840, asked the new School Board to take over responsibility for the schools.

The transfer was agreed and the existing Master and Mistress retained. Their salaries from January 1872 were recorded as:
- Master - £50 per annum, £20 in lieu of rent and rates, one fourth of the government grant and a sum equivalent to one fourth of the school fees.
- Mistress - £30 per annum, £15 in lieu of rent and rates, one fourth of the government grant and a sum equivalent to one fourth of the school fees.

Repairs and alterations to the school were agreed:

Boys' school - Room to be match boarded all round to keep off the damp and to avoid the necessity of painting, rearrangement of the classes and desks, a lobby for hats and coats constructed, flooring made good at the end of the room, new closets, lavatory, coke bin and ash pit.

Girls' School – New floor, rearrangement of the classes and desks, match boarding round the room as in Boys' School, new lobby for hats and cloaks, closets and lavatory.

The building in general to be cleaned and painted inside, south front to be painted and the words "Board School" substituted for "British Schools".

The contractor, Thomas Hellyer, was also instructed to widen the platform in the boys' schoolroom, repair, fit drawers and paint the Master's and Mistress' desks, to fix an iron-spiked rail to the south window and repair forms, to take away old desks and supply new tops in lieu of the same.

Thomas Hellyer attended the Board meeting on 24 January 1872 and was also instructed to execute the following:
- 48 iron stays to be fitted to desks
- Perforated zinc blend to girls water closet
- Wall in boys' yard to be made higher and glass bottles put on top
- Supports to be fixed to water taps
- Desks to be stained

- Zinc trays for umbrellas to be provided
- Gas to be fitted
- Socks to be fitted to drawers and desks
- Scraper to be fitted to girls' school door
- Weather board to be fixed

On 31 January 1872, the Clerk reported the alterations would cost £150. Thomas Hellyer was called on again for advice when the Rev Poole reported more ventilation was required in the Girls' School.

After consultation with Mr Jenkins, the School Master, the clerk of the Board was instructed to obtain the following supplies:

Boys – 10 dozen reading books, bible, copy books, slates and pencils, ink, ball frame, ink well tray, 4 dozen inkwells, map of the world, map of Africa, diagram of weights and measures, pictorial illustrations of geography (parts 1 to 6), visitor's book, hand bell, whale bone broom, hand brush, dust pan, pail, wood and coal (for both schools).

Girls – 12 dozen reading books, inkwell tray, 1 dozen inkwells, pictorial illustrations of geography (parts 1 to 6), swing slate, visitor's book, slates and pencils, picture of comparative sizes of animals, sheets of colour, form, letters and easy reading.

The first School Attendance Officer was appointed in 1872. Testimonials from several candidates were considered and after a ballot, three names were put forward:

- John Masters of Player Street, Ryde
- Henry Jenkins of Strand, Ryde
- Jacob Sibbick of West Street, Ryde

The clerk was instructed to draw up an outline of the officer's duties and his salary fixed at £25 per annum. There is no mention in the Minute Book which candidate was chosen. Part of the duties of the Attendance Officer was to visit families of absent children and find out the reason for the absence. Often this was due to illness, lack of money for the school pence (fees), the children having to stay home to look after the babies while the parents worked or the children themselves having to work to support their family.

The first school medals were awarded in 1874; boys' for general improvement; girls' for good conduct and general progress. In addition, a prize was awarded to the parents of a child in each school who attended most regularly, punctually and cleanly.

Evening School

In September 1874, the Ryde School Board recommended an Evening School should be opened for three nights per week.

Joseph Taylor, Master of the Boys' School, was asked to teach in the evenings in addition to his existing duties with an additional salary of £10 for six months plus half of the grant and half of the school fees. He had been appointed in January 1874 from St Ethelburga Society's School, London, and allowed 30 shillings travelling expenses and £5 towards moving to Ryde.

Joseph Taylor tried to increase the rate to £20 but settled for £10 after the Board initially refused his request. His salary was increased at a later date.

The only school log books for the evening school held at the Isle of Wight Record Office date from a later period of 1893 to 1895 and show during this time the evening school was for girls and they were taught cooking, domestic science (including how to budget), and arts.

Attendance and Discipline

Robert Fry was appointed School Attendance Officer in May 1877 and a uniform was provided for him: cap, coat (lettered School Officer), trousers, boots and gloves, Mr Wiltshire to supply the clothing and Mr Sansom the boots. The Minutes of the School Board show he was very often chasing the same parents and children for non-attendance.

The issue of discipline in schools is nothing new. Old log books show many children got into trouble in school, on the way to school and often played truant. Attendance would be low if it rained and on regatta days or when the circus came to town. If a holiday had not been given, many children just did not turn up!

In May 1877, the School Board decided a punishment book would be provided for each school. The Head Teacher was required to detail any problems and the punishment inflicted on the pupils.

This account from the Isle of Wight Advertiser dated 26 January 1878 shows pupils could end up in the Police Court:
"Ryde Police Court - Fred Smithers, a boy of about 12 living in Upton Road, was charged with assaulting Miss Phoebe Plaister, Head Teacher of the Bettesworth Road Board Schools. Complainant said that about 20 minutes before nine on the morning of the 11th inst. she was passing through Church Street, when defendant came behind her and threw the hood of her cloak over her shoulders and ran away. She said the other teachers had been positively afraid to pass that way to school on account of the boys insulting them."

No details of the punishment handed out to Fred was given in the paper.

Miss Plaistor married and moved to South Wales where she died in May 1905. Her obituary appeared in the Isle of Wight County Press on 27 May:
"News has been received in Ryde of the death at Penarth, South Wales, on the 9th inst, after a long illness, of Mrs Jones, who, as Miss Plaistor, was for many years headmistress, under the old School Board, of the Bettesworth Road School."

Even before this, the School Board Minute Book reveals an incident in October 1872. Augustus Leeds reported a girl misbehaved at the Board School and had been suspended by Miss Rowe, her teacher. He had been required to visit the girl and inform her if she repeated her bad conduct, she would be liable to be summoned for an assault on her teacher.

We are left to wonder what exactly her 'bad conduct' was and if any further action was taken. Her name is not mentioned in the Minute Book again.

Ashey Board School

Ashey Board School opened in Ashey Road, Ryde, on Monday 12 June 1876 at 10am. Miss Marion Bayne of Glynde, Lewes, was appointed Mistress and allowed £5 for the removal of her furniture to the Island.

The school, originally planned to take 50 children, was built to take 70 boys and girls following approval from the Education Department, Whitehall. The School Board requested plans be submitted from interested architects in February 1875 for:

"A Schoolroom for 70 children allowing a space of not less than 8 square feet per child; Classroom for 20 with a gallery, also no less than 8 square feet per child; water closet arrangement for a mixed school with separate playgrounds; a residence adjoining the school for the teacher. There must be no extraneous ornament of unnecessary expenditure incurred in the buildings."

Architects remuneration was the usual 5% on the outlay and an allowance of £5 was made to each unsuccessful competitor sending in plans.
On 11 March 1875, the Board accepted the plans drawn up by Francis Newman. They agreed the site should be fenced on the frontage with a brick wall 9 inches thick with coping and piers and a wrought iron gate.

Tenders for the erection of the school were received from
- Tom Saunders   £783-10s-0d
- George Henry Parsons   £784-0s-0d
- James Reid   £850-0s-0d
- Henry, Thos, & Hiram Jenkins   £750-0s-0d
- Leonard Potts   £788-0s-0d
- Charles Welch   £700-0s-0d

The Board recommended Charles Welch's tender to be accepted, being the lowest. The Clerk was directed to take steps for the insurance of Ashey School and teacher's residence for the sum of £600 in the Imperial Fire Office.

An estimate for blinds for the school was accepted on 4 April from A & W Coombes of 4 and 5 Monkton Street, Ryde:

"We agree to fit up complete eight rollers with Buff Holland Blinds, cords and tassels complete for the sum of £5-2s-6d. If fitted with Cope and Austin's Patent Furniture, 2s-6d per blind extra."

An order for desks, furniture and school equipment was made:

9 desks and forms with MacFarlane No. 3 standard tops, 1 ½ inches thick, stained and varnished, 3 dozen ink wells, 3 dozen ink well covers Macfarlane No. 2, 3 forms for the classroom, teacher's desk with cupboard, strong with chamfered legs and bottom rail, teachers table with one drawer to lock, 4 feet by 3 feet, book cupboard 4 feet high by 2 feet 6 inches wide, 14 inches deep with three shelves, rails for diagrams, wrought iron hat and cloak pegs, umbrella stand, 3 iron hoop scrapers, 2 bells, 4 mats, 6 chairs, fenders and screen, coal shoot and brushes, clock, dresser, plate rack, kitchen table with one drawer 4 feet by 2 feet 6 inches.

6 dozen Darnell's copy books (1 dozen each of Nos. 2, 4, 5, 6, 7, and 16), 3 exercise books, 1 box of pens, 1 box of chalk, 3 boxes slate pencils, ½ gallon ink, 4 dozen slates, 2 swing slates, 2 easels, map hook and 2 pointers, blotting and foolscap paper, maps of England, Europe and the world, set of pictures of animals, box of form and colour, lessons on form (1 to 5), letters and figures, lessons on colour, picture lessons in geography, Chambers Infant School reading sheets (Nos. 1 to 14), 2 sets of reading books "Stevens and Holes" and "School Board Readers", log book, admission register, registers and summary, bible, school fees book, stock and stores book, visitor's book, towels, dusters etc.

An inscription was to be put up:

"Ryde Board School Ashey School 1876"

Fees for the school were agreed at twopence per week.

The school closed in December 1916 and is now a private residence but the plaque can still be seen on the front wall of the house.

School of Art

The School of Art was established by Benjamin Barrow in rooms at the Town Hall in 1869. Income for the school came from the pupils' fees and the Department of Science and Arts, South Kensington, London.

Eventually a purpose built Art School was designed and built on the site of an old cottage at the Star Street end of George Street where the library now stands. The Crown Prince of Germany laid the foundation stone on 17 August 1874.

Bettesworth Road Board School

In 1875, Ryde School Board recommended a school be built in Bettesworth Road, Ryde. It was designed to take 180 boys, 200 girls and 220 infants.

Instructions were given to architects on 4 August 1875:
"To be erected on the corner of Church Street and Bettesworth Road; buildings to comprise a schoolroom and two classrooms to each department, with fittings and all the usual offices and playgrounds and a residence containing six rooms for the Master. Site to be fenced all round. An estimate of the cost must be sent with the drawings by 29 September 1875."

By October 1875, 37 designs had been received and three were selected to be put forward. The designs were open to inspection by the public on two days in the week commencing 14 October 1875.

On 19 October 1875, the Board received a letter from Charles Walker, of 12 Powis Road, Brighton, the owner of Fairlawn, Bettesworth Road:
"As the owner of the property, may I request you kindly bring before the notice of the Board at your earliest convenience, the serious depreciation which will accrue to my property, should this arrangement be carried out. One of my tenants, I may add, is an invalid and would be seriously incommoded by the close proximity of a playground. By the adoption of that arrangement by which the Master's house and garden are placed between Fairlawn and the playground and school, these inconveniences would be entirely obviated."

There is no note in the Minute Book to say if the plans were changed to accommodate Charles Walker's concerns.

These items were ordered for the school:
Boys –
- 12 desks each 12 feet 9 inches long for the schoolroom, Buff blinds, 4 gas pendants
- 3 desks each 12 feet 9 inches long for the classroom, 1 gas pendant, Buff blinds

Girls –
- 15 desks 11 feet 9 inches long for the schoolroom, Buff blinds, 3 gas pendants
- 3 desks 11 feet 9 inches long for the classroom, Buff blinds, 1 gas pendant

Infants –
- Buff blinds for the schoolroom, 1 gas pendant
- 6 desks 8 feet long for the classroom, Buff blinds, 1 gas pendant

Residence –
- 7 Buff blinds, 1 plate rack, 2 dwarf cupboards to the parlour 3 feet by 1 foot

Inscriptions –
- Round window Infants School – "Bettesworth Road Schools 1877"
- Over entrances – "Ryde Board School Boys", "Ryde Board School Girls", "Ryde Board Schools Infants"

The school opened on Monday 30 April 1877 and was destroyed in an air raid during World War Two in 1941.

Oakfield National School

Oakfield National School, School Street, was built in 1845 for 100 children with a residence for the Master, Mr H Young. The Infant School was added in 1856 and in 1870 it was enlarged by building an additional classroom.

In 1878 a new school known as Oakfield, St John's, was built on the site mainly from endowments under the wills of Lady C J and Colonel E V Harcourt. It could accommodate 442 children.

In the 1950s, two separate buildings were used on the site; looking straight ahead from St John's Hill was the school hall and older children's classrooms while the building to the right had three classrooms for the younger children. The boys and girls had separate playgrounds.

The school closed and was demolished to be replaced by flats.

Binstead National School

The school opened in 1853 to take 140 pupils under Master William Beale and Infant Mistress Miss Baker. It was enlarged in October 1871 by the architect Thomas Hellyer of Ryde, and again in 1897.

Holy Trinity National School

Holy Trinity National School was built in 1879 in Player Street, Ryde, to take 130 boys and 100 girls.

Mr G Jannaway, for a long time Assistant Master, was appointed Head Teacher of the Boys' department in September 1906 in succession to Mr J H Dixon who was appointed to the Oakfield Schools.

In 1924, a new mixed senior school was added to take 360 pupils. The Head Teacher was Miss K Hollis.

The school continued to take children between the ages of 5 and 15 until 1970 when The Comprehensive System was introduced on the Island. The school was known to many simply as Player Street School.

Gassiot Green Girls' School

Gassiot Green Girls' School was built in 1878 on land given by Charles Gassiot of Elmwood House, Tooting, Surrey, in memory of his father John Peter Gassiot. A stone tablet above the main entrance reads:

Gassiot School
1878
Given to St John's District Parish by
Charles Gassiot
Of Elmwood House, Tooting, Surrey
In memory of his father
John Peter Gassiot FRS DCL LLD
Late of St John's House in this Parish

John Peter Gassiot was a magistrate and distinguished scientist. He was also a member of the city wine merchants Martinez Gassiot and Co who also traded in Portugal. The company later became a subsidiary of Harveys of Bristol.

In 1951, the school became St John's Infant School and after an extension in 1968 became St John's CE Aided Primary School. The headmistress was Miss Wicks. It had three classrooms, two with a sliding partition that could be opened to create a school hall, and a dining hall. A grass area sloped steeply down towards Great Preston Road.

As part of the centenary celebrations in 1978, the Headmaster, Mr J Warne, planned a sports day, grand fete and a centenary mural to be painted on the playground wall. He also asked for memories of the school from old boys, girls and staff. Some of the letters he received survive in the school archives.

70

The sports day took place on Thursday 13 July 1978, in the grounds of Bishop Lovett School as the primary school has no sports ground of its own. The fete was held at the school on 15 July 1978.

Further extensions were made in 1992 and 1996 and a new entrance porch built in 1999. A new mural was painted to celebrate the millennium in 2000 with the children painting images of their own faces on the wall as part of the celebrations.

Upper Grade School

Upper Grade Boys' School opened in St John's Road, Ryde, in 1883. Situated between Benett Street and Riboleau Street it was built for 'higher and broader' education. Girls joined the school in the early 20th century.

In May 1905, the Isle of Wight County Press reported Mr P Allen, a former pupil of Upper Grade and of the School of Art, passed the examination of the Surveyors' Institute of Ontario in a highly successful manner.

The school remained on the site and became Ryde Secondary Modern, a mixed boys' and girls' school. Pupils passing the 11 plus examination went to Sandown Grammar School. The school closed when new buildings were built in Pell Lane, Ryde, later to become Ryde High School when the Island changed to the three tier comprehensive system.

Bishop Lovett School

Situated at St John's House, built in about 1769 for Colonel William Amherst, the school takes its name from Ernest Neville Lovett, the first Bishop of Portsmouth (1927 to 1936).

Previous owners of the house include a general, two MPs and an amateur scientist, John Peter Gassiot. Apart from a brief period when Sir Henry Thompson owned St John's between 1866 and 1871, the owners of the house have all come from just three families – the Amhersts, the Simeons and the Gassiots.

On 11 October 1945, a London property firm, Orten Estates Ltd, acquired the Estate and two years later, on 16 July 1947, they sold St John's House and grounds to the Isle of Wight County Council for £12000.

St John's became Ryde Church of England Secondary Modern School and, apart from the first floor that was converted into a flat for the Headmaster, the house and basement were used as classrooms and school dining hall. The first Headmaster was Mr V P Evans.

In 1970, shortly after the arrival of Mr J M Longhurst as Headmaster in September 1969, the Island introduced The Comprehensive System and the school became Bishop Lovett Church of England Middle School, as it remains today, taking pupils aged between 9 and 13.

Three new buildings have been added since 1951 to accommodate the growing school numbers and range of subjects taught today. The first in 1951 was the Practical Block consisting of two storeys with classrooms for science, arts and domestic science. Second was a long bungalow type building opened in the 1960s and the last addition, opened at Easter 1970, was the 'New Block' housing the main school hall, classrooms and kitchens.

The school had used an annexe in Green Street but the new buildings did away with that need and it is no longer part of Bishop Lovett School.

The grounds still contain poplar trees thought to be between 300 and 400 years old and rhododendrons, the first of which were planted in 1797 when Edward Simeon employed the famous landscape gardener Humphrey Repton to lay out the grounds. At the time, there were only 15 species of rhododendrons known to English gardeners.

Haylands Primary School

Haylands Primary in Playstreet Lane, Ryde, was the first school to be built on the Island after World War Two and was opened on Saturday 29 March 1947 by Miss May O'Conor, Chairman of the Education Committee.

The school was built to replace the Bettesworth Road school buildings, which were completely destroyed during the war by a direct hit on Sunday 22 June 1941. The children were given a temporary home in St Michael's Church Hall through the generosity of the vicar - they in fact stayed there for five and half years!

The new school built at a cost of £10,551 had light, airy classrooms and its own playground. New buildings were designed and completed in 1998.

Ryde High School

The High School was officially opened on 8 November 1963 in Pell Lane, Ryde. The opening ceremony was at 2.30pm and later from 6pm to 8pm, the school was open to the public with pupils showing visitors round the building including the new gym.

In June 1997, the school was the outright winner of a national award in The Times Educational Supplement's newspaper day competition. Its newspaper called The Correspondent was put together on the day by a team of 23 students. They beat competition from 460 other entrants and were awarded a plaque and a multi-media computer as a prize.

A specialist language and arts college, Ryde High School became a Community Language College in September 2000 and has its own performing arts theatre, Ryde Studio Theatre.

Roman Catholic Schools

In the 1850s, the Countess of Clare provided St Mary's Roman Catholic School in the High Street, (now the parish hall), paying the salary of two teachers. An elementary School, designed to take up to 64 pupils was opened in 1883 and in 1905, it was rebuilt to accommodate 72 children.

In 1902 The Convent of the Cross, a boarding school for young ladies at St Mary's Church opened. This school closed in 1989.

In 1924 a Roman Catholic school was opened in Appley Rise, the Lady Prioress being the headmistress. It closed before World War Two.

Private Schools

Many private fee paying schools operated in the town, some for day pupils and others taking boarders. Here are just two examples RSHG have been able to research.

Little Appley School

In 1897 Richard W Philpott, schoolmaster, took out a lease on a property at Appley Road, Ryde with the intention of opening it as a Boys' Private Preparatory School. It was previously leased by Robert Yelf, wine merchant of Ryde, and known as Sturbridge House.

With Charles J Pugh as joint headmaster, the school opened with just one pupil in October 1897. By the end of the term, it had four pupils. Numbers steadily increased to about 35 in 1920 and peaked at 70 after World War Two.

The school was known as Little Appley and the 1906 prospectus advises:
"The curriculum is formed with a view to enabling a boy who works honestly to take a good place at one of the Public Schools or at the Royal Navy College."

Many subjects were taught at the school including: English history, geography, arithmetic, algebra, geometry, trigonometry, Latin and Greek, French scripture, music, gymnastics, drill, games and PE, carpentry, manual work, acting and swimming instruction.

In addition, extra-curriculum activities included: butterfly hunts, walks on the downs, excursions, an air-rifle club, building tree huts, keeping pets and building forts. The school also published children's writing in a book called Stray Leaves.

Little Appley School had close links with the Royal Navy College established at Osborne House in 1903. From 1905, the college staff examined the pupils in French and maths, and in 1906, the school adopted the Osborne 'phonetic drill' in French. From 1908, they used the Swedish System of Physical Training used at both Osborne and Dartmouth Royal Navy colleges.

With the onset of World War One, the school undertook serious vegetable gardening and money raised from the surplus was given to charity.

A cadet battalion of the Hampshire Regiment (Isle of Wight Rifles) was established at the school in 1915. Of 81 'Old Boys' from the school of military age, (the oldest being only 30), 76 served in World War One. Sixteen of them died in the conflict.

Between them, the 'Old Boys' were awarded these medals:
- Victoria Cross (2)
- Military Cross (8 including 2 with bars)
- Military Medal (1)
- Croix de Guerre (3)
- Distinguished Service Order (2)
- Order of the British Empire (2)
- Italian Bronze Cross (1)

Charles Pugh retired as headmaster in 1920 and died in Cornwall in 1936 aged 73. Richard Philpott continued until 1929 when he retired after 32 years at the school. He died in 1946 aged 81 at Burford, Gloucestershire.

William Donovan Johnson BA, who had taught at the school since 1911, succeeded him as headmaster until 1933 when the Rev C E Squire MC MA was head. Kenneth S Mitcheson, who was later to share the duties with his twin brother Lieutenant-Colonel Philip S Mitcheson after he retired from the Indian Army, succeeded him in September 1938.

In 1940 with a number of the staff away on war service and after a plane crashed in an adjacent field, it was decided to open the school for the winter term at Wells House School, Malvern, Wiltshire, where Kenneth Mitcheson has previously taught for 10 years. The school returned to Little Appley in January 1942 after four terms away.

In 1964, with the declining health of the headmaster, declining numbers of pupils and growing financial pressures, closure looked imminent. Kenneth S Mitcheson exercised his option to buy Little Appley at this time for £6,000.

The school finally closed in December 1966. A final ceremony and presentation was held at Ryde Town Hall on Saturday 17 December 1966 attended by over 500 people associated with the school.

In the final school magazine, Kenneth Mitcheson noted all the records of the school since its foundation. They included bound copies of the school magazines, an honours board, photographs, films and tape recordings of the important occasions in the life of the school. He requested the records were passed to the County Archivist for safe keeping.

Kenneth Mitcheson retired to Merstone and died in 1973. His twin brother Philip continued to live in Ryde.

The Isle of Wight County Council purchased the house, grounds and playing fields from Kenneth Mitcheson in 1966 and sold Little Appley School and 2.94 acres of land in 1968 to the Lord Mayor, Aldermen and Citizens of the City of Portsmouth. The council retained a further 5.66 acres of land. The use of the property was restricted to educational purposes and the Isle of Wight County Council retained the option to buy it back in the event of it being sold within 21 years.

In January 1969, the City of Portsmouth College of Education appointed Mr W L Preece and his wife as wardens of Little Appley. It was used by students undertaking periods of practice teaching in Island schools and for field study courses.

Today the house is known as Appley Manor and is a privately owned restaurant. There are still pictures and adverts for the school on the walls inside the restaurant.

Ryde School

Ryde Grammar School, a private school, opened at Hanover House, George Street, Ryde, on 25 April 1921 for 46 boys. The first Headmaster was William L McIsaac who had led the discussions in December 1920 with local people on the need for a grammar school in Ryde. Mr McIsaac had previously been the headmaster of Upper Grade School.

In September of the following year, seven boarders arrived at Trinity House, the original boarding house of the school.

The Mayor of Ryde helped in the search for bigger premises and the school moved to Westmont, Queens Road, Ryde, in the summer of 1928.

In 1929, Examination success for a former Head Prefect was reported on 17 October 1929 in the Isle of Wight Times:
"Mr Crichton Merrill, a former head prefect at Ryde Grammar School, and son of Mr Charles Merrill of Lainston Grange, Appley, has passed the

Intermediate Bachelor of Law examination of the University of London. He was coached by Dr W G H Cook, of Southampton."

It became known as Ryde School from about 1931. In July 1971, the school celebrated its Golden Jubilee.

Today Ryde School, which merged with Upper Chine School formerly of Shanklin in 1994, is an independent co-educational day school for girls and boys aged between 3 and 18. The current headmaster is Dr Nicholas J England.

Fiveways, just across the road from the main school, is home to the Nursery, Reception class and Years 1 and 2 taking children from age 3 to 7.

The Junior School takes pupils from age 7 to 11, with the Senior School taking them through to age 18.

The school also has a number of boarders from the mainland who live on the campus at Bembridge, formerly Bembridge School, and are taken to Ryde each day in the school bus.

Other Schools

Many other schools have existed or still exist in the Ryde area but have not yet been researched by RSHG members and are not included in this chapter.

Some examples are:
- Swanmore Middle School, Bettesworth Road
- Partlands PNEU School (Parents' National Education Union), Partlands Avenue
- Mayfield Middle School, St Vincents Road
- Caversham House (now Dover Park Primary), Dover Street
- St John's Infant School, St John's Road,
- St Mary's Roman Catholic Primary School, Ampthill Road

There were also many private, and specialist music and language tutors in the town, operating mainly from rooms in their own homes. Some taught day students but others advertised as boarding schools for ladies or gentlemen.

Katharine Mary Osborne
1861 – 14/07/1930

She was a school governess with her sister Matilda at 7 Star Street, Ryde, in 1891.

In 1901, she was living at Summer Street, Willenhall, Wolverhampton, as the Principal of a private school.

She returned to the Island and was a valued worker at St Michael and All Angels Church.

She died aged 69 at Eastleigh, Ashey Road, Ryde, on Tuesday 14 July 1930.

Eleanor Barry
1859 – 08/01/1929

She was a Manager of the St John's Schools, Oakfield, for some years. Religious Education was a subject very dear to her heart and she gave loyal and devoted service to St Michael and All Angels Church.

She was well known and respected for her efforts on behalf of the general good of the community.

A lifelong resident of Ryde, Miss Barry died aged 70 at The Chestnuts, Ratcliffe Avenue, Ryde, on 8 January 1929.

Susannah Evans
1812 – 26/06/1893

Susannah Evans lived at Lind Street, Ryde, and was a former schoolmistress at the British Girls School in St John's Road, Ryde. Born in Deptford, Kent, she came to Ryde in the early 1840s. She was well known for her support for the cause of the Tichborne Claimant. She died aged 81 on 26 June 1893.

The Tichborne Claimant

Arthur Orton (1834 – 1898), who claimed to be the missing heir Sir Roger Tichborne (1829 – 1854) was an impostor living in Wagga Wagga, Australia, and became the subject of a celebrated 19th century legal case.

The real heir, the eldest son of a baronet and heir to the Roman Catholic Hampshire family of Tichborne, was drowned at sea when his ship was lost with all hands on its way home from Rio de Janeiro in 1854.

Lady Tichborne believed Orton, also known as Tom Castro, was her eldest son but after her death in March 1868, other members of the family found out he was actually a butcher's son from Wapping, London, who had jumped ship in Valparaiso, Chile, taking the name Castro.

A trial to establish his inheritance began on 11 May 1871. Orton was eventually convicted of two counts of perjury on 28 February 1874 and was sentenced to 14 years hard labour.

Harold Emanuel Bevis
1898 – 27/02/1924

Harold Bevis enlisted at Cowes in the Rifles Brigade, aged 17. He served in France in World War One, and was wounded and gassed, being discharged on 25 June 1918, aged 20.

He was nursed by his mother and often seen out in an invalid chair until his early death on 27 February 1924, aged just 26. She died of a broken heart on the day of his funeral.

Photographs of the school medal presented to Harold Bevis for Punctual and Regular Attendance by the Borough of Ryde Education Committee in 1909.

RSHG would like to thank Al Rowe for this contribution.

Gavin Hamilton
Died 18/05/1927

Gavin Hamilton graduated with first class honours from Oxford and became headmaster of Cranbrook Park School, London. He retired through ill health and came to live in Ryde in 1925.

He was a keen chess player and a member of the Vectis Chess Club. He also engaged in journalism and private coaching after retiring from his schoolwork.

CHAPTER 6

BREWERS OF RYDE

Esplanade Brewery

In the early years of the 19th century, shipbuilding was still being carried out on Ryde shore. One of the ship building companies was John and George Yates. Their workshops were to the east of George Street, but in 1829, they had disposed of the site to James Blake of Portsea, Hampshire, and he turned the workshops into a brewery.

Business must have been good around 1833 because he had a new brewery built on the site and a year later James purchased Frederick House, Castle Street. Five years later, he brought his son, Alfred Blake, into the business changing the name of the brewery to James Blake & Son.

In 1848, the property was put up for auction and George Clements of Southsea, Hampshire, purchased it. He was aged 43 and married with four children. It appears George Clements was not a 'hands on' man because in 1858, he advertised for a brewer to run the Esplanade Brewery.

In 1859, the family and the business suffered a terrible blow. George Clements was driving a coach, accompanied by his wife, through Vernon Square into Melville Street when the pony appears to have run away and he lost control. The wheel of the coach struck the curb in Melville Street and both passengers were thrown out. George Clements struck his head against the curb and was killed; he was aged 51.

In the December, the Brewery was advertised for sale together with nine public houses and one beer house. The business was purchased by W B & C Mew who closed the brewery and in 1860 sold all the fixtures and fittings.

The building was used as offices and stores until 1867 when Mews decided to move to the Green Dragon in Union Street and sold the old site to Kemp's Esplanade Hotel. Mr Kemp had the old brewery building demolished and extended his hotel in 1873.

John Cooper – Cooper's Brewery, Union Road

John Cooper was born about 1768 and married Jane Baker in 1796 when he was 28. They had a large family of which John junior was the eldest son. In the records available John senior is described as a blockmaker in 1791, a blacksmith in 1796 and a common brewer in 1801.

He owned a brewery known as Cooper's Brewery at the southeast end of Union Road. The property stretched from George Street through to Union Road on land he obtained in 1795 and 1800.

In 1801, Union Street was laid out, linking together the hamlets of Lower and Upper Ryde. Jane Player, widow of William Player, granted leases for buildings along the line of the new road and John Cooper built the first hotel in Ryde on the western side of this road, about half way up. Originally it was known as the Ryde Hotel, but three years later he sold it to Robert Yelf for £2,200 and ever since it has been known as Yelf's Hotel.

The building initially stood alone on the new road and was impressive enough to be the only inn in Ryde to appear in the 1811 edition of the Newchurch Parish Church Rate Book with the title "Hotell".

John Cooper died at the age of 48 in 1816 in somewhat strange and mysterious circumstances. He was found drowned in a vat of beer - whether he fell in drunk or was pushed was never discovered. It is said because it was not possible to lift his body out, the barrel was rolled out into Union Road where it was smashed open.

It is also said many of the locals stood by with pitchers and jugs to collect the beer as it spilled out of the barrel and ran down the hill!

After his death, Mrs Cooper ran the business until she died in 1850, and then her son John Cooper junior took over. He ran the business until his death, at his home, Denbigh House, George Street, Ryde, in 1865 aged 69.

The brewery and the four public houses associated with it were sold. The pubs were the Wheat Sheaf in Nelson Street together with a blacksmith's shop; the Oakfield Inn in Oakfield; the Barley Mow in Player Street and the Roadside Inn, Nettlestone, with the five tenements next to it. The brewery was closed down and the pubs were taken over by Edward Sweetman.

The Lake Family - Eagle Brewery, Star Street, Ryde

Eagle Statue above the former Eagle Hotel, High Street, Ryde

The Eagle Brewery was in Star Street behind the Eagle Hotel, High Street, Ryde. The owner was George Lake, son of William Lake.

George was born in 1799; he married Louisa, a Portsmouth girl, and had nine children. Their second son, George Worman Lake, took over the brewery upon the death of his father in 1848.

George Worman Lake lived around the corner in Stoke Cottage, 48 Star Street. He died after a short and painful illness on 4 March 1866 aged 38 and is buried in Ryde Cemetery. He had never married so the brewery and associated houses passed to his brothers, William and Harry Lake.

IN MEMORY OF
GEORGE WORMAN
LAKE
BORN APRIL 1 1827
DIED MARCH 4 1866
"May his soul rest in peace"
Amen

James Lake, the eldest son of George and Louisa Lake, was running his own business, The Lion Brewery, in direct competition at that time.

William and Harry set about building up the business. They decided to link their surname to some of the pubs, hence the Lake Huron, Lake Superior and later the Falls of Niagara to link in with the previous pubs.

In 1872 they decided to purchase Bank Cottage, in the upper High Street, it was pulled down to make way for a new public house called The Atlantic Tavern, which opened its doors for customers in the following year.

By his first marriage, William Lake had one child who died in infancy. After his first wife died William married Ann Isaacs, the daughter of Ryde butcher, James Isaacs, and they had one child who they named George Worman Lake after his deceased uncle. When he grew up George Worman's interest was in farming rather than brewing.

The brewery was hit with the death of William Lake in February 1877, aged 44 years, he is buried in Ryde Cemetery, and an even greater blow hit the brewery the following May, when his brother Harry Lake died aged 39 years; he is also buried in Ryde Cemetery.

In August 1877 the business was transferred from the executors of William and Harry to the widow Ann, but the previous month the whole business had already been put up for sale.

The sale included the following public houses: The Atlantic Tavern, The Partlands Hotel, Lake Huron, Weeks Hotel, Falls of Niagara, Lake Superior, and The Fleming Arms, all of Ryde, plus The Eagle Tavern, Ventnor and The Robin Hood, Brading. There was also an interest in a further five pubs and some dwelling houses.

Bidding opened at £10,000, it reached £20,800 and Edward Sweetman bid another £100 and became the purchaser. Sweetman already had the George Street Brewery nearby, so he closed down the Eagle Brewery and used the buildings for storage.

The Eagle Brewery passed into history except for the eagle statue on the top of the former Eagle Hotel that can still be seen in the High Street today.

Japeth Barton, Edward Sweetman Senior and the Sweetman Brothers. George Street – Star Street Brewery

In about 1836, Japeth Barton, a married man from Binstead, opened a brewery at 36 George Street. In 1853, he obtained land at the southwest end of George Street and a piece of the Star Inn's garden giving him access into Star Street. Five years later, he became bankrupt and retreated to Portsea, Hampshire, leaving his daughter Elizabeth to clear up the business.

Elizabeth sold the brewery to Edward Sweetman in 1861 and he carried on brewing at the premises, but William Baron Mew, a brewer of Newport, held the head lease. Later Japeth Barton came back to Ryde and died here in January 1866, aged 66; he is buried in Ryde Cemetery.

IN REMEMBRANCE OF
JAPETH BARTON
WHO DIED JAN 16TH 1866
AGED 66 YEARS

Edward Sweetman, son of Thomas and Mary Sweetman, was born in Ryde in 1827. Thomas was a tailor living in Union Road in 1846 and later lived in Buckingham Road. Edward married Elizabeth Sheppard from Kingston, Dorset, at St Thomas' Church, Ryde in 1847 and had eight children.

Edward's first brewery was established in 1848 in Buckingham Road when he was about 21. The nickname for the road at the time was 'Duck's Terrace'. It is thought the brewery was at the west end of the road near its junction with Spencer Road. The 1851 census tells us Edward and his family were living in part of Jordon Cottage, Buckingham Road.

By October 1853, he had moved to 5 The Colonnade, Lind Street. From there he moved to George Street when he took over the business from Japeth Barton.

Business was expanding and Edward controlled at least 18 public houses in the Ryde area plus some retailing outlets. The malt house was a large building situated between Daniel Street and Benett Street. In 1874, the brewery was rebuilt with the main entrance facing into Star Street and two years later, he purchased the Lion Brewery. Upon Edward's death in 1903, the brewery passed to his sons Henry, Charles and Walter Sweetman. His eldest son Edward junior was running his own brewery at the time and he was left a sum of money.

EDWARD SWEETMAN
BORN 30TH JAN 1827
DIED 15TH OCT 1903

The three brothers called the business H, C & W Sweetman, but the head lease was still held by the Mew family, brewers of Newport.

Charles Sweetman died in July 1920 at his home St Catherines, John Street. He had taken little interest in the brewery choosing instead a career in the volunteer army and he became a Major in the Royal Army Service Corps.

Henry Sweetman had an active interest in the brewery and was a partner with his brother Walter in Sweetman Brothers. He became a Justice of the Peace and, for 15 years, represented the West Ward of Ryde Borough Council.

He was also a Captain in the Isle of Wight Rifles. In the 1935 Jubilee honours he was bestowed a knighthood. Henry died at the Victor House nursing home, Partlands Avenue, Ryde, on 8 June 1944, aged 86 and is buried in Ryde Cemetery.

The remaining brother, Walter Sweetman, lived at Woodlands, Queens Road, Ryde. He was accomplished both as a musician and as a sportsman. He was a first class oarsman and at one time a champion on the South Coast and locally he played golf and bowls. As a musician he played in many Island concerts and was a member of the Ryde Philharmonic Orchestra. He was also a member of the Isle of Wight Rifles. He died suddenly in June 1943, aged 77, at a local nursing home and is buried in Ryde Cemetery.

In the early 1920s, with the depression and increasing competition from Mews and Brickwoods, the brothers decided to put the business up for sale. In 1920, Brickwoods made an offer of £35,000. For some reason this was not accepted and in 1921, they made a reduced offer of £30,000 on the condition the Sweetman brothers withdrew from the business.

W B Mew Langton made an offer of £30,240 plus £14,500 for the stock and this was accepted. Mews did not wish to brew in Ryde and closed the Sweetman Brothers brewery down. The building was used as a store and in 1935 it was demolished and replaced by the Commodore Theatre and Cinema.

Edward Sweetman Junior

Edward Sweetman junior was born in 1846, the son of Edward senior and Elizabeth Sweetman. He married Emily Shute of Southampton, Hampshire, who was 9 years younger than he was and they had seven children (6 girls and 1 boy). When he was in his late 20s, Edward acquired the Anglesea Brewery and ran it in direct competition with his father.

In 1878, Edward junior became the landlord of The Castle Hotel in the High Street and rented it for 21 years. About this time, he started to market soda water from premises in John Street. He also had premises at 137 and 138 High Street next to The Castle Hotel.

Over the years, Edward junior seems to have settled down in John Street making it his headquarters except for brewing which was still carried out at the Anglesea Brewery.

In 1885, he purchased Upton Windmill, Ryde, started to market chicken food, and became a corn merchant. A company, Messrs R Shute, was formed to look after this new business. Edward junior's wife's maiden name was Shute and the man managing the new business was Mr Shute, possibly a relation of hers. In 1915, Edward closed down the business and sold the windmill to Ernest Morey.

Upton Windmill

Edward's lease on The Castle Hotel expired in 1898 and it was purchased by Messrs G Gale & Co, brewers from Horndean, Hampshire, for £5,400.

The following year Edward purchased the Strand Hotel for £1,255. He closed down his business in John Street and moved his home and business to the Strand Hotel.

Although short of capital, he was still looking for new business ventures and in 1895 employed Ryde architect John Isaac Barton to draw up plans for a large new hotel in Swanmore Road. Total costs were to be approximately £4,000; nothing happened until 1900 when the site was cleared.

Edward's original plan was for a three-storey building, but the local authority objected and he submitted amended plans for a two-storey hotel. Building started in 1901 and the London Hotel opened for business in July 1902.

Soon afterwards, Edward's enterprises started to get into trouble. He had overstretched himself and by 1912 the business was in the hands of the Official Receiver.

A meeting was held in Yelf's Hotel, and a debtor's statement was issued showing Edward had a surplus of £79-7s-11d after settling his debts. He said he was losing £600 per annum by his trading. He and his family seem to have left the Island soon after this as no further trace can be found of them.

James Lake and the Duffetts - Lion Brewery, High Street

This brewery is first listed at 12 ½ High Street, Ryde, (now number 152) in 1852. The owner was James Lake, eldest son of George and Louisa Lake, owners of the Eagle Brewery. James had trained as a cooper and blacksmith, but decided to become a brewer and a rival to his father.

The business grew and James took his two eldest sons, George and Alfred Lake into the brewing business.

The family suffered several personal blows: first James' wife Betsey died in September 1871 aged 52; his third son, Edmund (or Edward) died in July 1875, aged 22; and finally his eldest son George died in April 1877 aged 28. All are buried in Ryde Cemetery.

After this James Lake lost interest in the brewery and in 1877 decided to put the business up for sale. James Garland Duffett sold his butcher's business in Ryde to Robert Morgan and purchased the Lion Brewery, where he carried on the business of brewing.

The Isle of Wight Times carried an advert announcing the change of owners. James Garland and his family lived at the Brewery yard and his wife Jane died there in 1879 aged 38 years.

In 1904, it was reported James Garland owned five public houses including the Beehive, Newport Street, the Rose and Crown, High Street and the Anglesea Tavern, Anglesea Street that he purchased in 1884.

James Garland Duffett died in 1909, aged 66 and is buried in Ryde Cemetery. His eldest son James George Duffett took over the business, he decided not to live at the Brewery but close by in Garfield Road.

JAMES GARLAND DUFFETT
DIED JANUARY 17TH 1909 AGED 66
"YEA THOUGH I WALK THROUGH THE
VALLEY OF THE SHADOW OF DEATH
I WILL FEAR NO EVIL FOR THOU ART
WITH ME THY ROD AND THY STAFF
THEY COMFORT ME"

In 1920 Portsmouth brewers Brickwoods started negotiations with James George Duffett, but business was bad, values were falling and there were problems over the property, so nothing came of the negotiations.

Mew Langtons also looked at it but refused to purchase the brewery and eventually it passed to Messrs Long & Co of Southsea, Hampshire. Longs closed down the brewery but kept the public houses. Sometime later Brickwoods bought out Longs.

James George Duffett retired in 1921 and went to reside at Beanacre, Ashey, and later to Wood Street, Ryde. He died in 1935 aged 69 and is buried in Ryde Cemetery.

JAMES GEORGE DUFFETT
WHO FELL ASLEEP ON DECEMBER 4TH 1935
AGED 69 YEARS
AT REST

Joseph Exton - Lamb Brewery, Brunswick Street

In 1851 a mariner named Joseph Exton, lived in Monkton Street with his family. A few years later the Exton's moved to Brunswick Street, (now Station Street) and opened a business as a brewery and beer retailer that by 1859 had become The Lamb Public House and brewery.

Joseph died aged 66 in 1866 and is buried in Ryde Cemetery. His widow Esther took over the business, closing the brewery but continuing with the public house. The brewery had run for only 11 years.

In 1870, Esther passed the public house to her son Henry James Exton and he ran it until about 1880 when Edward Pine became the new landlord.

Esther lived until 1879 aged 76 years. Her son Henry died in 1900 aged 66 years; both are buried in Ryde Cemetery.

SACRED
TO THE MEMORY OF
JOSEPH EXTON
WHO DEPARTED THIS LIFE
A......?1866
AGED 66 YEARS
ALSO
ESTHER, WIFE OF THE ABOVE
WHO DIED AUGUST 17 1879
AGED 76 YEARS
"HER END WAS PEACE"
(5 Lines of sentiment unreadable)

Ann Lowe and Thomas Richbell - Lower Union Road Brewery

This brewery was in business by 1839, also handling coal and corn. It was owned by Ann Lowe, widow of a prosperous grocer, William Lowe who died in 1818, and her son-in-law Thomas Richbell.

Thomas married Sarah Lowe, daughter of the widow in 1836. The 1841 census reveals Thomas came from the mainland and lived with his wife, who was born on the Island, in Walrond Cottage, George Street.

The directory of 1839 gives Castle Road as the home of the brewery, but this is probably incorrect, as all other documents relating to it quote Union Road as the address.

The plot of land extended from Union Road through to George Street. Ann Lowe lived in Walrond House and the brewery faced into Union Road.

It would appear Ann Lowe ceased to have any financial interest in the business as, in 1842 when Thomas Richbell was declared bankrupt, there is no mention of her, and the business was placed in the hands of local trustees.

Three years later, in 1845, the brewery was put up for auction. The adverts said it was a newly erected and compact brewery. Interestingly from a second advert, it would seem Ann Lowe, who now lived in Pier Street, did still have an interest in the property.

William Jacobs who lived at The Grove, Brading, purchased the business. In 1854, the brewery and the houses were again put up for auction. It seems nobody was interested and the business was closed down.

92

CHAPTER 7

TRANSPORT IN RYDE

The Promenade and Tramway Piers

The first view that many people travelling to the Island see is the lovely Victorian outline of Ryde with its pier reaching out into The Solent.

The pier itself has seen numerous changes in the last 200 years. It's hard to imagine Ryde without the Pier now but this early description of the approach to Ryde gives you an idea: "Between the sea and shore at low water there is an impassable gulf of mud and sand, which can neither be traversed by walking or swimming, so that for near one half of the twenty four hours Ryde is inaccessible by friend or foe".

Visitors from the mainland would be rowed as far as the sandbanks permitted and then carried piggyback fashion to the shore across the mud flats. Henry Fielding most famously described this in July 1754; he wrote, "I was at last hoisted into a small boat and being rowed pretty near the shore, was taken up by two sailors, who waded me through the mud and placed me on the land". Not a pleasant idea! Eventually a small pontoon was built.

In 1812, a group of prosperous estate owners and businessmen with a vision of the future realised the benefits to the town if it could be easily reached at all times of day and they formed the Ryde Pier Company. An Act of Parliament was passed allowing the construction of the pier.

The foundation stone for the Promenade Pier was laid on 29 June 1813 and it opened a year later on 26 July 1814. Before this there had been a boat service running from Portsmouth to Ryde, but it was not very efficient; it was restricted by the times of the tide making the disembarkation of passengers and goods difficult and at times dangerous.

The original timber pier, designed by John Kent of Southampton, Hampshire, was 1,750 feet long and 12 feet wide. It was extended in 1824 and again in 1833 bringing the overall length to 2,250 feet. It is one of the earliest public piers and the third longest in the country. The cost of building was estimated at £16,000.

A second pier was built alongside the existing Promenade Pier and opened on 29 August 1864. This pier had a tramway to take passengers to and from the Pier Head and Ryde Esplanade making the movement of passengers and goods much easier.

The original trams were horse drawn until 1885 when the lines were electrified. Petrol driven trams were introduced in 1927 and Drewry diesel railcars in 1959. The tramway finally closed in 1969.

In May 1876, approval was given to build a railway pier and a direct rail connection to St John's Station through a tunnel under the Esplanade and Monkton Street. In 1877, the work began on the third Pier.

Working on the pier was a dangerous job and there were several accidents reported during 1879. Six men were injured in March when the monkey engine and part of the pier staging fell into the water at low tide. Walter Buxey was the most severely injured when two pieces of iron fell on his chest; John Beavis had his leg amputated; Mr Clarke had his arm taken off and Mr Cousens was also severely injured. The other two men, Mr Newman and Mr Carpenter, although hurt, were able to walk home.

In July of the same year, in two separate incidents, Benjamin Hodges had his right foot crushed when the conductor started the tramcar without realising he was working underneath it, and a pile testing bar weighing a ton struck George Sutton. He was taken to Ryde Infirmary with serious injuries.

On 12 July 1880, at a cost of approximately £250,000, Ryde Pier Head Station opened, together with the line to St John's Road Station. The Pier Head had three timber-planked platforms, all over 400 feet long and a timber canopy to protect the passengers from the weather.

The tunnel, an incredible feat of engineering, under the Esplanade and Monkton Mead allowed the railway to reach St John's Road Station. The engineers overcame extreme difficulties and hazardous conditions due to the depth of the silt deposit and nature of the soil the tunnel had to be driven through.

Completed in 1881 and still in use today, the tunnel is 396 yards (362 metres) long and the tunnel descent, part of which is below sea level at high tide, is 1 in 50. To allow trains to enter the tunnel, the exit from the Esplanade Station had to be a sharp left curve so the track ran parallel to the Esplanade.

In October 1908, the pumps in the tunnel failed and it flooded. It took a week to pump out.

Owing to the increasing popularity of the Island as a tourist destination, the Esplanade Station soon became the busiest on the Island. It was continually bustling with people travelling from the mainland and local people going to other stations on the Island.

Postcard of Ryde Pier Head c1910

The Pier Head went through a series of enlargements starting in 1827, when it was expanded to allow two steamers to berth. It was also a place of entertainment; a music license was granted in 1841 and a band played in the summer months.

In 1842 James Langdon, contractor of Ryde, enlarged the Pier Head and a small pavilion and shelters were built at a cost of £400.

In 1895 a concert pavilion, later known as the Seagull Pavilion, was built on the Pier Head under the direction of John Isaac Barton, an architect and later Mayor of Ryde. It was a domed, octagonal two-storey building with a concert hall, reading room, refreshment room and an upstairs sun lounge. This proved to be a great source of enjoyment to the people of the town. It has since been demolished.

In June 1924, the Southern Railway Company bought Ryde Pier and during the 1930s, they rebuilt the Pier Head in concrete. The tracks increased from two to four lines but in 1966 reverted to two. The pier signal box, just to the north of the Esplanade Station, was demolished at this time and all signals on the pier and Esplanade were operated from St John's Road Station. In 1976, Ryde Pier was made a grade II listed building.

Although parts of the Pier have changed over the years, much of the original structure remains and some of the fine wrought-iron work can be seen along its length. It is still a busy working pier and is a credit to our town and its people.

The Victoria Pier

About 200 yards east of the Promenade Pier, the Victoria Pier was built in 1863 and was locally known as The Penny Pier due to the 1d tolls. It was funded jointly by the Stokes Bay Pier and Railway Company and the Isle of Wight Ferry Company to link the new Gosport ferry service from Stokes Bay, to Ryde.

Built to 970 feet, it was originally meant to be the same length as the existing pier but disagreement between the companies and the Town Commissioners together with a shortage of funds restricted its length. It opened in 1864 but with an infrequent ferry service and the tide restrictions, business was very disappointing. Part of the structure was damaged in a gale and the shareholders, in financial difficulty, were forced to sell it to the Ryde Pier Company in 1865.

The Victoria Pier was then used as a bathing station with public baths erected at the Pier Head and a free bathing stage at the shore end. Hot and cold ozone baths were advertised in 1876 with tickets costing 6d each. It was very popular until the end of the 19th century when the custom declined. An Act of Parliament allowed its demolition in 1916 and the remaining traces were washed away in 1924.

The Promenade Pier with the Victoria Pier in the background

The Tramway

Opposite the end of Cornwall Street is Cornwall Street Slip, and the promenade curves landwards to meet the Esplanade. A tramway passed over the Esplanade at this point on its way to join the railway at Ryde, St John's Road, via a smaller station in Simeon Street.

The tramway, a horse-drawn service begun in 1864 when it ran solely the length of the Pier, increased in length by degrees and lasted until early 1880 when through services to St John's Road ceased. The tramway system retreated to running the length of the Pier and remained so until the last tram met the last boat on the night of 26 January 1969.

In order to reach St John's Station, an ingenious scheme had to be resorted to. Ryde Corporation had objected to the trams running along the roads, and also the Monkton Mead Brook runs under Cornwall Street, which was the obvious route.

The Tramway Company bought three houses along Strand to the west of Cornwall Street and ran the tracks across their back gardens. To avoid passing along Cornwall Street they made a tunnel through the ground floor of the eastern most house, Holywell House, and the tramway went through that!

It was reported passengers were advised not to stand up while passing through the house, where there was a clearance of just seven feet!

Holywell House from Strand showing Tramway tunnel

St John's Road Station

Opened in 1864, the station was the terminus for the Isle of Wight Railway line from Shanklin that opened on 23 August 1864. It was also used by the Isle of Wight Central Railway, for their trains from Newport via Smallbrook Junction.

The railway was not allowed to start from the Esplanade because of the number of level crossings needed to cross the town. Approval had been given to build a terminus in the Melville Street area approximately ¼ mile away from St John's Road but the railway company decided to stop at St John's Station where they had already based their headquarters and workshops. This left passengers with a mile to travel to reach the pier.

In 1871, the horse tramway was extended from the Esplanade to St John's Road for the benefit of passengers with onward journeys.

In July 1865, the Isle of Wight Railway tried and failed to get the necessary permissions to cross St John's Road by level crossing. The original Act of 1860 specified a bridge should be built and the Town Commissioners insisted this was to be the case. The bridge was eventually built in 1880 with the line to the Esplanade.

The signal box at St John's Road was originally located at Waterloo East Station, London. It was dismantled and brought to the Island where Southern Railways rebuilt it in 1928.

Ryde St John's became the main depot in 1957 when Newport shed and workshops closed. Locomotive sheds west of the station were demolished after the withdrawal of steam trains in 1967. Workshops to the east continued to be used by British Rail.

The Tramway Pier running rails were removed and the Pier Head station incorporated into Ryde Pilot Office, leaving little trace of the Tramway between the Esplanade and St John's Road station.

A small interchange station was built at Simeon Street in 1876. It was never used for trains as inspectors considered the signalling arrangements inadequate, and also did not feel comfortable with horses and steam trains working alongside each other. Part of the station building survived and was incorporated into garage buildings but now houses have been built on the site and another part of our heritage has been lost.

John Harrington's 'ARAB' Bicycle

In the 1870s, John Harrington was building 'The Arab' bicycle at his bicycle works in Union Road, Ryde. The Arab was a High Wheel Bicycle. This type of bicycle, also sometimes referred to as The Penny Farthing, consisted of a small rear wheel and a large front wheel that pivoted on a simple tubular frame, both wheels had tyres of rubber.

The Arab

The advantage of the large front wheel was the distance that could be achieved with a single rotation of the fixed pedals. The High Wheel bicycle proved very popular among young men of wealth and reached the peak of its popularity during the decade of the 1880s.

Because the rider sat high above the centre of gravity, if the front wheel should be stopped suddenly by hitting a stone, bump in the road or other obstruction, the entire machine turned forward on the front axle, and the rider, with his legs trapped under the handlebars, was dropped forward on to his head!

Over the years, John Harrington put his name to several dozens of patents mostly to do with bicycle construction.

He eventually moved his business from Ryde to Coventry although some castors and castor bowls continued to be made in Ryde by Harrington Patents Limited in a workshop situated between the old St James' Place and Garfield Road.

A liquidation sale of stock and machinery on Friday 13 July 1900 ended the Harrington connection with Ryde completely.

Edward Tom Ward's Cycle Making Business

Edward Tom Ward first set up his bicycle making business in Ryde around 1878 when he was in his mid 20s. He and his wife Eleanor lived in Monkton Street and they had six children, four boys and two girls. By 1901, Edward was employing two of his sons, Edmund and Edgar, in his manufacturing business.

Edward Ward was a pioneer of cycling on the Island. He was one of the first members of the Vectis Cycling Club and an original member of the Cyclists Corps attached to Princess Beatrice's Isle of Wight Rifles before World War One.

By 1910, the business, Edmund Ward & Co, had expanded to include cycle makers and agents, motor engineers and a domestic machinery depot, and it developed into a flourishing motor and charabanc trade.

As a young man Edward Ward was a chorister at the Wesleyan Methodist Chapel in Nelson Street and later at Garfield Road Methodist Church.

In later life, his main recreation was a small sailing boat and he took part in races of the old Amateur Sailing Club, whose headquarters were on the pier. He was also one of the oldest members of the Ryde Conservative Club.

He died at the age of 86 years, on 12 December 1938, at 43 Melville Street, Ryde, after a long illness. His wife Eleanor died 22 years earlier.

Two of his sons also predeceased him; Corporal Edgar Ward of the Machine Gun Corps died at Passendale, Belgium, on 21 September 1917 aged 33 years, and he is buried in the New Irish Farm Cemetery, Belgium; Edmund Ward died in Ryde in 1924 aged 45 years after a long illness.

Edward Tom Ward memorial

Ryde Carriers

Carriers plied their trade around the Island for many years. They transported, delivered, collected, bought and sold, and would take passengers to and from wherever they wanted to go.

A customer would indicate they needed a carrier's service by post (a more regular and reliable service in those days!), by word of mouth or by 'The Flag' which was the more usual method.

Because a carrier had a regular route, and passed at regular times, a flag made of a stick and a rag, or piece of cloth would be attached to the front gate, stuck in the hedge or left at the end of the lane leading to the customer's house. If two carriers passed along the same route, each would have his own specific coloured flag. In the early days, horses pulled the vans.

The journey could be very uncomfortable with passengers often having to help push the van up a hill come rain or shine. For many it was the only way to travel. With the coming of motor transport, the journey might have become more comfortable, but there were still times when a little help was needed on the steep Island roads.

In the 1850s Ryde was already an established and thriving town with its own trade and shops. People did not need to travel to market to sell their goods or obtain supplies like those in more rural communities, while larger hauliers such as Curtiss and Pickfords and the new Ryde to Newport railway generally carried merchandise from the growing port of Ryde.

Carriers in the Ryde area started operating more local services from the villages of Bembridge, St Helens, Seaview and Nettlestone.

In 1850, there were only a couple of services operating between Newport and Ryde. George Beazley was one; he operated a route from the Rose and Crown, St Thomas' Square, Newport, to Ryde. Mr Vanner also operated along this route. Few other carriers are recorded following this route until the turn of the century when Mr Tutton left daily from 160 High Street, Ryde, to the Rose and Crown, Newport.

Leonard Dyer, using The Castle Hotel as his base, covered the route between Seaview, St Helens and Ryde before World War One. William Harvey also ran a daily service.

Henry Burden started before the war and continued afterwards trading as Burden and Coombes.

The trade between Ryde and Newport started to increase after World War One, when some returning soldiers invested their gratuities in the new motor transport that was becoming more reliable and efficient, Ford's Model T becoming the standard one-ton vehicle used by many carriers.

Arthur Orchard operated between Ryde, Brading and Bembridge from the mid 1920's but sold out to Gerald Price in 1930. Walter Dimond was operating the Ryde to Newport route about 1924 and the Millmore family also ran a regular service in the 1920s.

Martin Millmore ran his business from the corner of West Street and Green Street. He sold his business to Christopher Matthews, an ex-Regimental Sergeant Major in the army, who built up a successful trade between the wars. He, like other Ryde carriers, often had to park to the side of the Church in St Thomas' Square, Newport, as the Square was full of rival carriers. Christopher died in 1946, and his son, Leonard Matthews, who had been a driver in the Far East during World War Two, took over the business and traded as C G Matthews & Son.

He drove daily to Newport, one of his regular calls being Quarr Abbey where he delivered the fish he collected from the railway station. An important part of his business was delivering building supplies for Duke Brothers builders' merchants who did not have their own transport. Due to his deteriorating health, Leonard began to concentrate on more local furniture deliveries, much of which was for Dibbens of Ryde, his light brown van becoming a familiar sight in the town.

In 1963 he sold the business to Dibbens, who at that time were buying out several of the Island carriers, chiefly to acquire the coveted 'A' licences introduced by the Road Traffic Act of 1933.

The carrier trade had started to decline during the 1930s when the legislation was introduced to protect and control the transport service. Competition from regular bus services helped end the passenger service the carrier had provided for many years.

Later legislation prevented unregistered operators from carrying people, finally making the carrier service unviable.

After World War Two transport and railway services were nationalised delivering the final blow to the carrier's trade, which reached its unavoidable end in the 1960s.

The Stage Coach

The Stage Coach was a familiar sight in Ryde. Until 1890, the coach Civility, built by R B Chiverton of Newport for Abraham Vanner, made two daily trips from Ryde to Newport and back.

Civility would collect her passengers from outside the Lion Hotel on the corner of Garfield Road, Ryde, and could carry about 16 people fully loaded.

Broderick postcard about 1906 Ryde
This postcard in not the Civility but shows a similar coach

The first stop was at the tollgate by the brook forming the boundary between the Brigstocke and Fleming Estates near Binstead. Next was the Sloop Inn, Wootton tenanted by the Vanner family. Two of the lead horses would be uncoupled and stabled here if the coach was lightly loaded.

Abraham Vanner passed the Sloop Inn to his daughter Jemeley who married Frederick Purkis in 1865. Their two sons Albert and Fred carried on the family tradition driving Civility on her daily trips.

As the railways and roads improved, the tourist trade increased. The Vanner family began excursions by horse-drawn charabancs. They took up to 20 people at a time to popular destinations along the sea route to Ventnor, and to Carisbrooke Castle and the famous watercress beds nearby.

During the summer season, full day trips to Alum Bay stopped at the Eight Bells Inn, Carisbrooke to change horses and for refreshments.

The transition from horse to motor cars effectively put an end to the horse-drawn business. Vanners' horses and carriages were laid up at Stonepitts Farm and at a coach house in Union Lane, Ryde. They were eventually sold off for the small sum of between five to ten shillings each.

Civility was stored at the coach house until 1929 when, in conjunction with the Schneider Trophy air race, Abraham Vanner was asked by the Isle of Wight County Press to bring her out of retirement to travel once more her familiar routes.

Schneider Trophy Programme 1929

The scene was somewhat different to the old days when Civility travelled along the quiet country lanes – now cars and vans took to the roads and aeroplanes flew overhead.

The stagecoach passengers, dressed in period costume, must have looked out of place even on this special occasion. William Moul provided the horses and Les Moul, of Rosemary Stables, Ryde, took the reins aged only ten.

Pilot Henry Waghorn in a Supermarine S.6, a single-engine, single-seat racing seaplane, won the Schneider Trophy 1929.

The coach, back in retirement in Union Lane, stood at the back of the garage for many years and her interior used to store paints. Her current resting place is unknown.

The Paul Family
Owners of Ryde's first Motor Coach Company

The Isle of Wight County Press dated 1 February 1930 reported the death of Harry Paul, aged 78, who for many years had been a well-known businessman in Ryde. Harry Paul had started in business on his own as a haulage contractor and Post Master. Before the introduction of the steamroller, he had supplied a team of horses for pulling the old-fashioned road roller in the town, while for tourists he provided wagonettes and brakes for touring the Island.

His son, also called Harry, joined him in the business. While serving in France during World War One, he became interested in the new motor transport when he was posted to one of the newly formed Tank Corps delivering ammunition to the front line. Being shrewd businessmen, they saw the wisdom of adapting to the new mechanical transport, and quickly introduced charabancs and motor vans into their business.

When Harry senior died in 1930, his son continued to run the business, and encouraged by his wife, established himself as the owner of Ryde's first motor coach firm, Pauls, running many excursions around the Island. Harry junior died in 1968 aged 80, leaving two daughters and two sons. Both Harrys are buried in Ryde Cemetery.

Harry Paul senior memorial

Harry Paul junior memorial

Harry and Elizabeth Williams

Harry Williams was born in 1858 at Dudley House, John Street, Ryde, one of eight children. His father, George Williams, kept a posting yard with horses and stately carriages so characteristic of the mid-Victorian period. Harry owned his own horse and chaise at a young age and by the age of 18 was a fully-fledged licensed carriage driver.

On 2 November 1880, Harry married Miss Elizabeth Nippard at the Wesleyan Church in Ryde. He was 22 and she was 18 years old at the time. Elizabeth was born in 1862 at Hythe near Southampton, Hampshire, but moved to Brading with her parents when she was only a small child and from the age of 13 years lived in Ryde. She was brought up in a family of nine children.

For seven years, Harry and Elizabeth Williams lived at the Old Brigstocke Mews situated at the lower end of Church Lane and then moved to 8 Church Lane where they spent the rest of their lives.

Five of the couple's sons fought in the army in the First World War, two of them George and Sydney, were killed in action, and a third, Arthur, was badly injured. Private George Henry Williams of the Hampshire Regiment was killed on 8 November 1914 aged 35 and is commemorated on the Ploegsteert Memorial near the town of Leper, Belgium. His brother Sydney Harry Williams of the Royal Garrison Artillery Unit was killed on 14 September 1917 aged 30 years he is buried in Mendinghem Military Cemetery also near to Leper, Belgium.

Harry and Elizabeth celebrated the sixtieth anniversary of their marriage on Saturday 2 November 1940 and on that day, they reminisced about their lives together in Ryde. Harry had taken visitors on tours of the Island in his coach and horses in the time when it took three or four days to complete the 'Round the Island trip.'

"Excursions used to be run each weekend from London," said Mr Williams, "I would set off on Friday with four passengers in the carriage, with sometimes one horse and sometimes two. After driving leisurely through the woods and chines and avenues lined with trees, we would put up for the night at Blackgang Hotel. Then the next day we continued our journey, and spent the night at Alum Bay Hotel, returning to Ryde on Monday. When, as was often the case, I had nice people the trip was enjoyable, and I was able to point out the various things of interest. Sometimes the people were a bit grumpy, and I let them get on with it and did not talk overmuch. The weather in those days was much more seasonable, and we never got summer weather in the winter as we do nowadays."

He once had the honour of driving HRH Princess Beatrice and Prince Henry of Battenberg from Ryde to Seaview in a pair-horse landau.

In one respect, Mr Williams admitted the "Good Old Days" were not so good. "The roads were all gravel," he said, "and we had to flatten down the roads with our horses' hooves and carriages. Just when we had got one side of the road nicely levelled off the road authority would place barriers across it forcing us to start all over again and wear down the fresh gravel on the other side. Later they had a roller drawn by six horses."

Both Harry and Elizabeth Williams could remember Ryde in the days when the railway from Ventnor reached only as far as St John's Road. There was no railway to Newport, horse drawn trams plied up and down the pier. They used to walk on a long since demolished structure known as The Penny Pier. "Ryde's policemen wore top hats in those days," said Mr Williams with some relish.

IN
REMEMBRANCE OF
HARRY WILLIAMS
DIED JUNE 2nd 1941
AGED 83 YEARS
ALSO ELIZABETH
WIFE OF THE ABOVE
DIED MAY 10th 1945
AGED 83 YEARS

"HE BRINGETH THEM UNTO THEIR
DESIRED HAVEN"

Frederick William Chessell
1876 – 1963

Frederick Chessell of 10 Cross Street, Eastfield, Ryde, died on 5 September 1963 aged 87 years, just 16 days after he and his wife had celebrated the 65th anniversary of their wedding at St John's Church.

Frederick Chessell was born at St Helens and spent his whole life in the district.

He drove some of the Island's first motor taxis and worked for one taxi firm for more than 40 years. During World War Two, he drove for the War Department at Puckpool Park.

He worked at Parkes cycles' business in John Street, Ryde, until a year before his death. Mrs Elizabeth Chessell lived for another 8 years and died in 1971 aged 95.

Robert Reed
1819 – 1899

He lived at Allswell Cottage, Belvedere Street, Ryde, and was a coachman to Dr Bloxham from 1855 to the doctor's death in 1868.

He then worked for Dr Davey until the day of his death on 11 August 1899.

George Henry Humber
1870 – 1949

He was a coachman in 1901 working for Hugh Meares of Millfield House, Queens Road, Ryde. George lived at the Coach House Rooms next to the house.

George Henry Humber, of 45 George Street, Ryde, died aged 79 on 28 December 1949.

Walter Herbert Ernest Jolliffe
1870 - 19/01/1939

Walter Jolliffe, one of the three original tram drivers on Ryde Pier, died at his home, 1 St John's Wood Road, Ryde, on 19 January 1939.

He began working for Smith and Sons, stationers, when he was 14 years old before leaving to work on the pier. His last position was tram driver. He retired about 1934.

CHAPTER 8

MARITIME HISTORY

Ryde's Maritime History

Being a coastal town Ryde has a rich maritime history.

From Medieval times, the hamlet of Lower Ryde was one of the Island's main ports, and even before Ryde became a town, the inhabitants made their living by fishing, boat building, piloting vessels, and providing transport between the Island and the mainland.

The townsfolk of Ryde will have witnessed many Fleet Reviews in The Solent at Spithead dating back as far as the 14th century. A Fleet Review is a British tradition where the monarch inspects the massed ships of the navy. It originally occurred when the fleet was mobilised for war, or for a 'show of strength' to discourage potential enemies. Since the 19th century reviews have often been held for the coronation of a monarch or for special royal jubilees and have often included delegates from other national navies. Forty four naval reviews have been held to date and because they require a natural large, sheltered and deep anchorage, they have often been held in The Solent at Spithead and in full view of Ryde.

Ferry Services between Ryde and Portsmouth

The transporting of people, goods and later vehicles between the mainland and the Island via Ryde has clearly played an important role in the development of the town.

In about 1420, the lord of the Manor of Ashey set up a ferry service controlling the boats that crossed from Portsmouth to the fishing village of 'Ride'. In the 1600s, there was a requirement for fishermen to make a crossing to Portsmouth and back when requested. Failure to comply would result in a fine, so a rota was established with sailings as frequent as every two hours in the summer time. Eventually a special type of sailing boat called the Ryde Wherry replaced the fishing boats. In 1796, the first purpose built ferry entered regular service, it was a large sailing boat called The Packet and made the crossing between Ryde and Portsmouth twice a day.

The first steamship service to the Island started in 1817 with The Britannia, making the trip twice a day. The service was later withdrawn as the vessel was found to be unsuitable for The Solent waters.

In 1825, the paddle steamer PS Union entered service carrying wheeled vehicles and livestock as well as foot passengers and two months later PS Arrow joined her. In 1826, a third ship PS Lord Yarborough was introduced and a fourth ship, PS Earl Spencer, was added in 1833. The Portsmouth and Ryde Steam Packet Company owned all the steamers.

By 1842 as many as ten sailings per day operated during the summer between Portsmouth and Ryde.

In 1880 up to thirteen sailings a day were made from Monday to Saturday with five sailings on Sundays. The service thrived and by 1912 increased to twenty six sailings a day, with six modern steamers in service.

742 cars were shipped between Portsmouth and the George Street slipway in Ryde in 1913, but the First World War brought severe cutbacks to this service. Four of the six steamers were requisitioned as minesweepers during the war and in 1918, only 48 cars were shipped across the Solent on tow boats.

Over a million people were carried on the Ryde Pier service in 1923 and over 100 cars were carried on the Ryde tow boat service. 1925 was the last full year of the tow boat operation between Portsmouth Harbour and Ryde Esplanade, nearly 2,000 cars were carried. The following year the tow boat service moved from Ryde to a new slipway at Fishbourne Creek and the total of cars carried across the Solent reached almost 4,000.

In 1927, the first car ferry service was launched making two return crossings between Portsmouth and Fishbourne daily. In 1930 two large paddle steamers, were purpose built in Scotland and brought to the Island. They could carry 1,183 passengers and were mainly used for summer excursions and cruises. An additional ship was added to the fleet later the same year, but the three ships found it difficult to meet the demands of the new service. On summer weekends, they made 15 round trips between them.

PS Ryde

In 1934, a slightly smaller ship was built for the day-to-day run between Portsmouth and Ryde Pier. The paddle steamer PS Ryde entered service in 1937. In the same year, 24,000 cars were carried on the service between Portsmouth and Fishbourne.

Between 1939 and 1945 two of the ships, MV Fishbourne and MV Wootton were commissioned for military service as minesweepers. Both vessels were involved in the Dunkirk evacuations; although they both reached France, they were not used to carry any personnel back to Britain.

Diesel ships were introduced after the war and by the mid 1950s, the Portsmouth to Ryde ferry service was in its heyday. On the August Bank Holiday of 1956, over 60,000 people used the route in one day. Since the end of the war, it had not been uncommon to see queues of people on a Saturday stretching the whole length of Ryde Pier and sometimes even reaching up Union Street! The three diesel ships and three paddle steamers could not cope with the demand and fishermen would tout for trade at the side of the pier offering to carry passengers back to Portsmouth.

MV Shanklin

In the 1960s the car ferry service was improved, an hourly service was maintained and foot passengers were carried on that route for the first time. By 1967, with improved vessels, the demand increased considerably and 274,000 cars and 24,000 freight vehicles used the car ferry service that year.

Towards the end of the decade, further improvements were made to the fleet crossing The Solent and on 13 September 1969 the paddle steamer PS Ryde retired from service; she went briefly to London and then returned to a berth at Binfield on the River Medina. She became a nightclub for some years but for many years now she has been quietly falling apart. For a long time it had been hoped she could be restored and brought back to her former glory but she is now beyond economic repair and is a sad sight at Island Harbour, Binfield near Newport.

During the 1970s, further improvements were made to the car ferry and by the late 1970s, a 24 hour service could be provided. The terminals in Portsmouth and Fishbourne struggled to cope with the volume of traffic and a new ferry terminal was built in Portsmouth on the site of the old Gunwharf power station. The new terminal opened in February 1982 although the terminal building was still under construction and did not open until 1983.

In 1980 MV Shanklin, the least mechanically sound of the three diesel ships providing the service between Portsmouth and Ryde Pier, was withdrawn from service. She was sold to The Waverley Trust as their Prince Ivanhoe but in 1982, she struck rocks off the Welsh coast and was lost. The two remaining diesel vessels struggled to keep up with demand and a catamaran, the Highland Seabird, was chartered and used as an experiment on this service.

Construction of the Fishbourne linkspan began in late summer 1982. 78,000 cubic metres of material were removed from Wootton Creek to widen and deepen the channel in readiness for the next generation of vessel.

In the winter of 1982, there were problems at Ryde due to the withdrawal of MV Shanklin. A replacement vessel, the car ferry MV Freshwater, was drafted in from the Lymington route, but she was far from ideal.

At peak times passengers had to squeeze into the small accommodation or stand on open decks. As a temporary solution, two redundant single decker buses where loaded to provide accommodation and somewhere for the passengers to sit during the crossing.

MV Freshwater on the Ryde to Portsmouth passenger route
Photograph courtesy of David Marshall

Another high speed experiment was tried on the Ryde passenger service in the summer of 1983 with the introduction of the hovercraft Ryde Rapid that made daily crossings between Ryde Pier and Clarence Pier, Southsea, Hampshire. This was a fairly successful experiment, but only on calm days!

At the same time the biggest ferry to serve the Isle of Wight, MV St Catherine, entered service between Gunwharf and Fishbourne. She carried 142 cars and 1,000 passengers. Accommodation in the form of bars and plenty of deck space was provided above the car deck and a crossing time of 35 minutes was maintained. Later the same year her sister ship MV St Helen took the title, weighing in at 2983 gross tonnes. In 1987 a third super ferry, MV St Cecilia was added to the fleet and in 1990 a fourth, MV St Faith.

In 1986, the passenger ferries on the service between Portsmouth and Ryde Pier were replaced with high speed catamarans from Tasmania. The two vessels provided accommodation for 470 passengers and were able to make the crossing in 15 minutes. A twenty minute frequency was maintained during the summer months.

The last diesel ship made her final crossing between Ryde Pier and Portsmouth on 11 September 1988, retiring after 40 years of service. In 2000, two more catamarans were purchased for the Ryde Service and they shared the route with the 1986 built craft.

In 2001 a new, larger Polish built ship, MV St Clare, entered the car ferry service on the Portsmouth to Fishbourne run, able to carry over 180 cars and 770 passengers and providing accommodation in the form of superior lounges, bars and decks for the passengers.

Ryde Lifeboat

In February 1869, the need for a Ryde lifeboat became apparent. During a gale the schooner W S Flowers ran aground on Ryde Sandshead, the five crew members held on to the rigging for over two hours. The Ryde Coastguards of the day saw what was happening and in their small four-oar rowing boat set off to rescue the crew. With the assistance of people on the sands and other craft, the Coastguards were able to save the lives of all the crew. This incident highlighted the need for a lifeboat for Ryde, and Thomas Dashwood, the Mayor, put out a call to all interested parties to meet and discuss the issue.

Although the meeting was not well supported, it did include a representative of the Pier Company who, with the permission of his directors, put forward the idea that the pier could be used as a place to have the lifeboat stationed. Also at the meeting was a foreman sent by Messrs Lamb and White, boat builders of Cowes, to give technical advice. The meeting agreed a lifeboat was needed and an advert was placed in the Isle of Wight County Press asking for subscriptions to enable a lifeboat to be purchased.

Captain Hans Busk by H J Fleuss

Augustus Leeds, JP, had the idea to approach a gentleman called Captain Hans Busk. He had been responsible for originating England's Volunteer Army and a testimonial had been forwarded to him in respect of his work in this field. Captain Busk however had graciously declined to accept the money.

Augustus Leeds suggested to Captain Busk the money could be used to purchase the lifeboat for Ryde and he readily agreed to this idea. An order was placed with Messrs Lamb and White to build the lifeboat to be called the "Captain Hans Busk".

A management committee was set up to oversee the project and they estimated the running costs of the boat would be about £20 per year. The committee agreed this sum could easily be raised from subscriptions.

On 5 May 1869, the boat came by road from Cowes and was met at the site of the proposed new Parish Church in Queens Road, Ryde, by an escort of the Isle of Wight Rifle Volunteers, Coastguards and the crew from HMS Marten. Crowds of people lined the way for this momentous occasion as the boat was taken down to the pier.

The lifeboat was thirty feet long, six feet wide and two feet four inches in depth with two masts. It was made of Spanish mahogany and seasoned wych elm; she came equipped with everything needed, including cork life jackets for the crew, sails, two sets of oars and anchors.

There was a handing over ceremony and the Captain Hans Busk received a rapturous welcome. Lady Ranfurly launched the lifeboat, and there was a salute from the guns of HMS Marten anchored off the pier. The boat exercised in front of the crowds of onlookers. Later there was a dinner at the Pier Hotel where a plaque commemorating the launch was unveiled. The plaque was later placed next to the lifeboat station on the pier.

The First Rescue

In September 1869, the first gales since the introduction of the Ryde lifeboat were seen. The sixty-ton cutter Volante started to drag her anchor.

A watchman on the Pier Head raised the alarm but could not awaken the crew of the Volante to the impending danger. The lifeboat crew were called to the pier and the lifeboat, The Captain Hans Busk, was launched.

The Volante was already heading past the eastern pier and the crew were on deck and aware of the dangers when she ran aground. The crew clung to the deck and rigging as the yacht was hit by continuous waves.

The damage to the vessel was severe and it was a race against time in perilous seas that The Captain Hans Busk struggled to save the lives of those on board.

Despite the early hour and severe weather, people stood all along the pier straining their eyes through the storm and willing on the brave souls who were risking their own lives to save others. Finally, The Captain Hans Busk made contact with the Volante, and its crew were quickly transferred to the safety of the lifeboat, which pulled back on its anchor to get clear of the danger.

After transferring the nine survivors of the Volante to safety, The Captain Hans Busk went on to save a further eight lives from other vessels in danger. She spent over nine hours during the raging storm helping others.

The crew members for this famous first rescue were Henry Southcott, coxswain, Mr T Howard, 2nd coxswain, John Gawn, Thomas Gawn, Samuel Southcott, Mr H Cotton and Edward Burnett.

Other crew registered to the boat were Mr C Osmond, Mr W Howard, Mr R Fry, Mr E Perkiss and Stephen Sivell.

The Selina on Southsea Beach the day after the tragedy

On New Years Day 1907, the Selina Lifeboat was called out to assist a man who was seen to be struggling in a rowing boat off Dover Street slipway.

The Selina left Ryde at about 5:30 pm with the full complement of crew on board: William John Bartlett, coxswain, George Jeffery, bowman, Ernest Cotton, Alfred Linington, senior, Alfred Linington, junior, Daniel Reeves, Albert Reeves, Henry Heward, second coxswain, and Frank Haynes, commissioned boatman of Coastguards. They searched for some hours without success.

After talking to the Warner lightship and finding no more information, they decided to return to Ryde. The sea was choppy and the weather squally. As they were returning to the Pier, the Selina was struck by a sudden and heavy wave and capsized immediately throwing her crew into the icy cold water.

The crew held on to the hull of the boat as best they could and cried for help. They drifted for several hours in the cold and the dark and finally, as the boat drifted near to Southsea, PC Vines, a policeman on duty, saw her and summoned the Coastguard. The survivors were rescued although in an exhausted state.

As they were being rescued, it was found that Coastguard Frank Haynes and fisherman Henry Heward were missing. Their bodies were recovered the next day.

The man they set out to rescue had managed to scull across The Solent landing opposite Eastney Barracks, Southsea, earlier the same evening. It would appear at no time was he ever in any real danger.

The funeral of Frank Haynes and Henry Heward took place in Ryde the following Monday afternoon and was attended by huge crowds of people who lined the streets and literally filled the cemetery.

The funeral cortege, passing through Pier Street and Union Street to St James' Church, was led by a firing party of the Coastguards from the Cowes Division who marched with arms reversed. Flags were flown at half-mast at the Town Hall, the Pier, the Coastguard Station and the Castle as well as at many private houses, while shutters were up and blinds down along most of the route.

The Funeral Procession in Lind Street

After the service at the Church, the procession reformed in Lind Street that was thronged with people. The service was made more poignant by the presence of a little white coffin containing the body of Frank Haynes' three month old daughter, Edith Louisa Haynes, who predeceased him on 30 December 1906.

The Church bell rung out as the long line proceeded through the High Street and Hill Street to Ryde Cemetery.

The Rev R R Cousens gave an address at the graves that were side by side, three volleys were fired and the Last Post sounded. The crowd slowly filed past the graves in a mark of respect for the gallant lifeboatmen who perished in the terrible tragedy.

The graves of Frank Haynes and Henry Heward
marked by headstones and an anchor

Floral Tributes at the funeral of Haynes and Heward, 1907

The Prince of Wales Pleasure Boat Tragedy 1856

On Thursday 11 December 1856, The Prince of Wales pleasure boat, belonging to John Wearn, left Ryde at 3pm for Southampton, with a party of gentlemen on board. It had been a stormy day, but as the weather improved, the boat started out on its return journey to Ryde.

Shortly after midnight, as the boat neared the Menelaus lazaret, (a ship set apart for quarantine purposes), which was anchored at an area of The Solent known as The Motherbank, the weather turned stormy once again, and the boat capsized.

Fortunately, the men on duty on board the lazaret heard the crew's cries and immediately lowered a boat and hastened to the rescue. They managed to save two of the men, George Austin and Charles Wearn. Unfortunately, one young man named, George Page, also known as George Stone, drowned before he could be rescued.

Due to the continuing bad weather, the boat was only recovered and brought back to Ryde on the following Sunday. The Isle of Wight Observer dated 20 December 1856 reported, "She was found all sails standing and sheets fast, which does not indicate watchful seamanship". The rough weather also scuppered all attempts with trawls and drags to recover the body of George Page at that time.

In response to the tragedy, a subscription was opened for the benefit of the seaman's widow, at Mrs Wagner's library in Union Street, to which Sir Augustus Clifford, Sir James Caldwell, Sir John Burgoyne, and many others of the gentry contributed.

When George Page's body was eventually recovered from the sea, an inquest was held on 18 May 1857 at the Vine Inn before Mr F Blake, coroner. The body of the 31 year old seaman was only identified by his clothing, his wages for the day still in his trouser pockets.

The evidence given by the two surviving crew members demonstrated George Page had died accidentally, and the jury returned a verdict of "Accidental drowning" accordingly.

George Page was buried at St Thomas' Church, Ryde.

John Gawn - A Local Hero
Gave his Life to Save Two Children

John Gawn

John Gawn of Ryde was Mate of the schooner Corinne.

The yacht left Cowes on Saturday 7 September 1889 and headed westward to anchor at Totland Bay.

The cutter, with a crew of five men, put out from the yacht for a sail in Scratchell's Bay. On board were the nephew and niece of the owner, Chas Goschen.

A sudden gust of wind capsized the boat and there ensued a terrible struggle for life in the strong tide.

The rest of the crew swam for their lives but John Gawn took the children, aged 14 and 9 years, in his arms and swam with them for some twenty minutes.

A fisherman in a boat nearby, heard the cries for help, and rowed to Gawn's assistance. He reached them just in time to save the children. As soon as the children were released from Gawn's grasp, he fell back exhausted and sank. He was pulled into the boat and attempts were made to revive him, but it was too late.

Another yachtsman in the boat, Mr Lind of Poole, Dorset, was also drowned but the other men were saved by clinging to the oars. The children were in an exhausted condition but survived.

At John Gawn's inquest, the jury placed on record their high appreciation of his conduct, and at the same time, some surprise was expressed he received no help from his comrades.

His funeral took place at Ryde Cemetery on Thursday 12 September 1889 conducted by Rev A H Delafield. There was a large gathering of friends and members of the Forrester's Court. The polished coffin was covered in wreaths sent by the Goschen family, his comrades from the yacht, and from Sir John Lees of Beechlands, Ryde, (where Mrs Gawn was engaged).

HMS Royal George

HMS Royal George, launched in 1756, became the flagship of the Channel Fleet during the Seven Years War against France and Austria.

At 200 feet long, she weighed 3,745 tons, and carried 100 cannon. Her quarterdeck rose 32 feet above the sea and her three masts extended to 100 feet in height.

In 1759, she triumphed in the Battle of Quiberon Bay where the French Fleet was defeated. In August 1782, the Royal George sailed to join the fleet at Spithead to relieve Gibraltar from the blockading Spanish forces. She was now the flagship of Rear Admiral Richard Kempenfeldt, under the command of Captain Martin Waghorn.

To allow minor repairs to a submerged water cock and with no time for dry dock in Portsmouth, the captain decided to heel the ship over by seven degrees at sea. Normally ropes would be attached to the masts and the ship pulled over from another vessel. Captain Waghorn decided instead to move the cannon from one side to the other causing the ship to heel over.

A carpenter reported water entering the gunports and requested an order to "right ship". It was some twenty minutes after she began to sink Captain Waghorn gave the order to reposition the cannon. By this time, it was too late. She capsized and sank in the middle of the Navy's Solent anchorage on 29 August 1782.

There had been 820 crew and a further 400 visitors made up of friends, family and trades people on board the ship in addition to 548 tons of stores and 83 tons of ammunition needed for the expedition. Reports say there were only 300 survivors.

Rear Admiral Richard Kempenfeldt drowned in the tragedy. Many bodies were washed ashore at Ryde and buried in the area of today's seafront Canoe Lake and Strand.

HMS Sirius was the flagship of the first fleet to set sail for Australia.

The Fleet left the Motherbank, between Portsmouth and Ryde, on 13 May 1787 and arrived in Port Jackson, Australia, on 26 January in the following year.

In October 1788, she was sent from Port Jackson to the Cape of Good Hope to get provisions for the colony that was on the brink of starvation. The voyage took over seven months. She sailed to what is now known as Mosman Bay to be repaired and refitted, and stayed there until 12 November 1789.

In March 1790, she was wrecked on the reef at Norfolk Island while landing stores and it was almost a year before her crew were rescued and returned to England.

To mark the 200th anniversary of Europeans arriving in Australia, the Mosman Council in New South Wales commissioned three identical bas-relief sculptures of HMS Sirius, from the sculptor Alex Kolozsy; one was presented to the residents of the Borough of Medina and the other two are at Mosman Bay in Australia and Norfolk Island in the South Pacific.

The Borough of Medina sculpture is in Appley Park, Ryde, opposite Appley Tower. The Mayor of Mosman, Alderman Peter C Clive, Aldermen B S J O'Keefe and D C Brockhoff and Mr V H R May, Town Clerk, travelled to the Island from Australia for the unveiling ceremony performed by Lord Mottistone, CBE, Lord Lieutenant of the Isle of Wight on 29 June 1991.

Captain Wallace Martin Caws
Cunard - White Star Lines Choice Pilot

IN
AFFECTIONATE REMEMBRANCE
OF
BLANCHE
THE DEARLY BELOVED WIFE OF
WALLACE MARTIN CAWS
WHO PEACEFULLY PASSED
AWAY
JULY 28th 1933
AGED 59 YEARS
"UNTIL THE DAY BREAKS"
ALSO OF
WALLACE MARTIN CAWS
DIED JUNE 5th 1948
AGED 73 YEARS

Captain Caws was a member of an old Island family that had an association with the Pilot Service for over 200 years.

In 1741, Anthony Caws settled in Seaview and purchased property in the High Street. He was a pilot and each succeeding generation supplied members to the service.

Wallace Martin Caws was one of three sons of Captain Samuel Caws who became pilots. He was apprenticed to his uncle and granted his licence in 1900. In 1908, he was appointed senior choice pilot for the American Line that became the White Star Line some five months later. He retained the position for the next 25 years and piloted some of the world's largest ships.

In May 1908, Captain Caws piloted RMS Adriatic, the largest ship in the world at the time, on her maiden voyage; he was one of the youngest pilots in the service, testimony to his great seamanship.

He piloted RMS Olympic in 1911 on her maiden voyage and took charge of the ship until the end of her career. Captain Caws joined RMS Titanic at Belfast when she made her first voyage to Southampton in 1912 and was in charge of the bridge when she came through from the Nab Tower to Southampton. He also piloted her sister ship, RMS Britannic, which was lost during World War One.

In 1922, he went to Cuxhaven, Germany to join the ship SS Bismarck, granted to the United Kingdom by the German reparations. She was renamed

RMS Majestic by the White Star Line and was the largest ship in the world at the time. Captain Caws piloted her into Southampton no less than 200 times.

After further promotion, Captain Caws was appointed choice pilot by the United States Line in 1933 and he had charge of the SS Leviathan, formerly the German ship SS Vaterland. About the same time he was appointed to a similar position, when the Cunard and White Star Lines amalgamated, succeeding his cousin, Captain Neil Greenham, of Seaview, who retired from the Cunard vessels.

Added to his responsibilities were the large vessels, RMS Berengaria, formerly the German SS Imperator, RMS Aquitania, and RMS Mauretania.

RMS Berengaria was taken over by the United Kingdom as a war reparation, and in 1920 purchased by Cunard and White Star lines jointly. In 1921, she entered Cunard Line service. In 1938, RMS Berengaria was sold for scrap after a fire at New York.

Postcard of RMS Berengaria passing through the Fleet at Spithead

Captain Caws piloted RMS Queen Mary through Spithead on her maiden voyage in 1936 and on a further 71 occasions until the outbreak of World War Two. By all accounts, the Queen Mary was his favourite because he said she was so easily handled.

Although he never piloted RMS Queen Elizabeth, he was closely associated with the arrangements for her historic dash to New York from The Clyde, Scotland, early in World War Two. The British Government let it be known she was possibly going to Southampton and every official who would normally take part in handling the ship was taken to the Clyde. When RMS

Queen Elizabeth left a week later, the officials were quietly taken off the vessel and instead of heading for Southampton, she made for New York avoiding the submarines waiting near St George's Channel which connects the Irish sea and the Atlantic Ocean between Ireland and Wales.

On completing 40 years service, Captain Caws received a presentation from the Brethren of Trinity House. Three years later, he retired and was succeeded by Captain James Bowyer of Ryde.

Wallace Caws, a keen gardener, was a member of the Borough of Ryde Allotment Association Committee, a sidesman and a member of the Parochial Church Council at All Saints Church. He was also a member of the Chine Lodge of Freemasons, the Sir Arthur Holbrook Lodge of Mark Masons and Ryde Bowling Club.

Captain Wallace Martin Caws died at his home, Seacroft, Queens Road, Ryde, on Saturday 5 June 1948, aged 73.

His funeral was held at All Saints Church on Tuesday 8 June 1948. The Vicar, Canon A Cory officiated. He is buried in Ryde Cemetery.

Present and past Trinity House pilots attended. Also present were representatives from the Southampton Pilot Service, the Masonic Lodge, Isle of Wight Bowling Association, Ryde Bowling Club, All Saints Parochial Church Council, the Island division of the St John's Ambulance Brigade, Cowes Bowling Club, Ryde Allotments Committee and the Bembridge Harbour Master.

RMS Queen Mary

Captain James Stallard
Smuggler

Revenue Cutter chasing
smuggling Lugger

James Stallard was born in St Helens in about 1796. As a young man, he was apprenticed to Pilot Beazley who was known as 'Old Razza Beazley', but soon after his service ended, he entered into the business of smuggling.

In those days, smuggling was thought by many to be an honourable profession, as long as one managed to escape detection of the authorities and from the commencement to the end of his career James Stallard evaded or outran all the revenue cutters.

In order to be a successful smuggler an intimate knowledge of the coast was essential and Stallard possessed this knowledge to a remarkable degree. His first small but swift vessel was named The Fox, it was once chased by a King's cutter, the commander of which was sure he could make an arrest, but the crafty smuggler hoisted up a keg of brandy on the mast, ran his vessel near a dangerous reef of rocks, tacked, and soon left his pursuers miles astern.

The Fox was once seized in harbour, but as no positive proof of any illicit traffic could be produced, the authorities had to give her up. Stallard had an even faster vessel named The Sun, which he was induced to sell to Mr Green, a large ship owner for a considerable sum of money with which he purchased The Gem, also a fast sailing yacht.

As the old revenue sailing cutters were superseded by steam vessels that Stallard knew he would not be able to outrun, he wisely decided to retire from his illegal activities, and for a while, he contented himself with an income from letting his yacht to gentlemen fond of cruising.

The discovery of gold in Australia gave a fresh impetus to the restless mind of the old captain and, together with his eldest son, he planned a voyage in The Gem to Australia. They entered into an agreement with a man named Mr Capel, well known in Ryde, to convey him to the distant colony. The venture proved to be an unsuccessful one for Stallard whose son was struck down by fever in Melbourne, where he died, and he was compelled to dispose of The Gem for considerably less than it was worth in England.

On his return to the Island James Stallard endeavoured to settle down and make a living running a public house in Hill Street that he named after his favourite vessel, The Gem. The pub was commonly known as The Undertakers' Arms because of its close proximity to the cemetery and Ellery's the stonemasons.

Stallard would often spin a yarn to his many customers about his former days when good French brandy was 'cheap'. No amount of reasoning could persuade him there was anything wrong with smuggling or any damage was caused to the community by evading the tax upon spirits. He argued that if the Government needed money, they should find something else to tax.

Although he was sometimes funny and agreeable, James Stallard was by no means a pleasant man, he was often close and disagreeable and, as the infirmities of old age came upon him, he became somewhat churlish. Stallard had been a widower for many years, but a few months before his 75th birthday he took a young wife. The union was, apparently, not an entirely happy one, and a few days before his death the old man pitched the young woman out of a window. Whether he was drunk or mad at the time was never discovered.

When Stallard died a few days later there was an inquest into his death, and, at the request of Stallard's son, the young wife did not attend. Stallard had made a will in favour of the young woman and the son thought his death might have been brought about by means not entirely fair.

The Coroner heard Stallard and his wife occupied separate apartments, and early in the morning of 7 June 1872, the old man had been found by his wife lying on the floor of his room quite dead. After a long enquiry, the jury came to the conclusion his death was caused by apoplexy and a verdict to that effect was recorded.

The Gem Inn, Hill Street, Ryde.

CHAPTER 9

NATURAL HISTORY
IN RYDE CEMETERY

Trees and Shrubs

Ryde Cemetery is home to a huge variety of plants, some planted on purpose as part of the design and layout of the cemetery but many are self-seeded. The largest plants are the trees; some of them may be more than 150 years old, surviving from the original planting scheme carried out in 1863 by Mr F Cooke of Newport.

Copper Beech Trees

The Isle of Wight Gardens Trust surveyed all the mature trees in the cemetery in 1999. They numbered and plotted them on an Ordnance Survey digitised map. RSHG has transferred this information onto one of our new cemetery maps and both the map and the list of trees are available to download from our website www.rshg.org.uk.

The 1866 Ordnance Survey map shows a dense planting of trees lining all the paths in the cemetery, with the exception of the Old Parish Cemetery section. The number of trees is now greatly reduced but Irish Yews still provide the basic framework of the planting.

Irish Yews are a traditional tree found in cemeteries and there are many in Ryde Cemetery, most of which are fruit bearing female trees.

A number of theories exist as to why the Yew tree is so common in churchyards and cemeteries. Some people say it is because of the dark foliage symbolising sorrow; others say it is because the tree is so poisonous it signifies death and possibly resurrection; yet others say it was put in cemeteries where it was inaccessible to livestock, and grown there to provide wood for longbows. For eons all over Europe, people have considered the Yew as 'The Tree of Life'. Yews can live for a very long time, over a thousand years, and they have come to symbolise immortality.

At the western end of the cemetery along the boundary with Pellhurst Road is a shelterbelt of pine trees and shrubs. There are a large number of self-seeded ash trees that have grown between the stones of monuments, and have caused considerable damage. The Weeping Ash, also found, is said to symbolise sorrow and also the fountain of life.

There are two impressive Deodar (Himalayan) Cedars, one to the north of the central chapels and the other to the south next to the boundary with Adelaide Place. The name Deodar is derived from the Sanskrit word "devdar" meaning "timber of the gods".

Deodar Cedar in Flower November 2007

In the sunken northeast corner, there is an enormous and magnificent specimen of Bay that is probably self-seeded. It has engulfed several monuments of 1879 - 1880 and is now a feature of interest in its own right. This tree measures 28m 50cm around the basal circumference, the branches come right down to the ground.

There are many species of shrubs in the boundary hedge and throughout the cemetery, including Euonymus, Privet, Elder, Bramble, Dogwood, and Hawthorn, several species of Laurel, Cotoneasters, Griselinia, and Hydrangea.

One notable species is the 'Hedgehog Holly', in the northern boundary hedge. This fascinating plant has shiny leaves that have a creamy white margin and spines not only on the leaf margins but also on the leaf surface. Holly trees are found throughout the cemetery and many are heavy with berries in the autumn and early winter.

There are many rose bushes; most of them planted on graves as a token of remembrance. Some have been left un-pruned for years and sprouted from the old rootstock to create a single plant with different coloured roses, and an abundance of hips in the autumn.

Autumn Berries 2006

Flowers

The cemetery was developed on farmland and meadows; it has had minimal interference over the years and not been subjected to intensive cultivation. Apart from regular strimming of the grass, annual hedge cutting and the occasional clearing of graves, the soil is mainly untouched by pesticides and weed killers. This means it is home to an abundance of flowering plants, bugs and insects.

In springtime whole areas of the cemetery, particularly the Old Parish Cemetery and along the southern boundary, are carpeted with Primroses and Bluebells that make a beautiful sight.

Several recommendations have been made, by different groups, for specific areas of the cemetery to be left natural and uncut to permit the full range of species to grow and seed. Some visitors may see this as unsightly, but the benefits of developing these 'islands of natural habitat' could outweigh the appearance of neglect.

In spring 2007, RSHG members found a few examples of the Green Winged Orchid in the cemetery. This plant would certainly be encouraged and will increase in numbers if allowed to grow and seed over the spring and summer.

Green Winged Orchid 2007

Throughout the spring and summer the flowers in bloom include: Bittersweet, Black Meddick, Birds Foot Trefoil, Bristly Ox Tongue, English Bluebell, Bugle, Common Cleavers, Common Vetch, Cow Parsley, Cowslip, Cuckoo Flower, Cut leaved Cranes Bill, Dogwood, Elder, Evergreen Alkanet, Field Bindweed, Field Madder, Germander Speedwell, Herb Robert, Honeysuckle, Knapweed, Laburnum, Lady's Bedstraw, Meadow Buttercup, Mouse eared Hawkweed, Oxeye Daisy, Perforated St John's Wort, Pink Sorrel, Plantain, Primroses, Quaking Grass, Red Clover, Salad Burnett, Scarlet Pimpernel, Sheep's Sorrel, Slender Speedwell, Spear Plumed Thistle, Three Cornered Leek, White Stonecrop, Wild Thyme and Green Winged Orchid.

Butterflies and Moths

Because of the wide variety of plant life and the sheltered conditions of the cemetery, it is also home to an array of butterflies and moths.

In July 2006, RSHG hosted a Butterfly Walk in Ryde Cemetery, led by Richard Smout. The species seen on that one day included several Meadow Browns, a Comma, a Speckled Wood, a Red Admiral, and an unidentified white butterfly, as well as a Yellow Shell Moth. In addition, a Damsel Fly was seen, and Hover flies and Bees were in abundance.

We have also seen Peacock Butterflies, Holly Blues, a Dagger Moth and a Six Belted Clear Wing Moth.

Six-Belted Clear Wing Moth July 2007

Peacock Butterfly July 2007

Animals and Insects

The cemetery is home to many animals and insects including: flies, spiders, snails, woodlice, ants, slow worms, bees, wasps, beetles and ladybirds, to name a few.

Slow Worm May 2006	Yellow Snail 28 May 2006

On warm nights in the spring and summer, hedgehogs can be heard going through their courting and noisy mating rituals. In the autumn and winter, they often find shelter in the garden of The Lodge, no doubt attracted by the many slugs or the dog biscuits sometimes left out for them.

Fox

On winter nights "unearthly screams" can sometimes be heard coming from the cemetery. You could be forgiven for thinking there might be ghosts and ghouls about, but a more likely explanation is it is the mating call of a vixen fox that lives there.

Although the foxes are often heard and occasionally their scent can be detected they are rarely seen. In 2002, a fox skeleton was found under a large bay tree.

Birds

In the cemetery, many birds are seen overhead, as well as resting and feeding on the various plants and nesting in the trees and shrubs. The berries, insects and caterpillars provide an attractive food source for many species and their young.

On spring and summer evenings, it is a delight to walk in the cemetery and listen to the bird song. Although it is close to the centre of town, it is far enough away from roads and traffic for the bird song to be enjoyed.

Green Woodpecker

In the spring when the sun rises early in the morning, the birds respond to the first light with the 'dawn chorus' all joining together in song to welcome the new day.

The dawn chorus occurs as winter retreats and male songbirds sing to attract potential females, protect their territory and to warn off other males.

As soon as it is light enough to look for food, the dawn chorus comes to a close, which is why you have to be an 'early bird' to hear it.

We have seen a Green Woodpecker, Magpies, Blackbirds, Robins, Wrens, Blue Tits, Great Tits and Coal Tits, Green Finches, Dunnocks, Chaffinches and Pigeons; a Jay was spotted in 2006. Although their numbers are declining, many Sparrows can still be seen and heard.

Sparrow

Blackbird

138

Huge varieties of fungi grow within the boundaries of Ryde Cemetery. Although different species of fungi can be found in the cemetery at all times of the year, the best time for searching is in the autumn.

In October 2006, RSHG hosted a "Fungi Foray" lead by Jackie Hart, a member of the Isle of Wight Natural History Society. Unfortunately, it rained on the day, but a few hardy volunteers turned up and accompanied Jackie on her interesting and informative walk through the cemetery. Rain does not help in identifying fungi as it spoils the cap colours.

Jackie collected up a basket of different finds that she took away and these were later identified as:

- Agaricus campestris - Field Mushroom
- Agaricus silvaticus - Blushing Wood Mushroom
- Agaricus xanthoderma - Yellow Stainer Mushroom
- Boletus luridus – Lurid Bolete
- Boletus porosporus
- Coprinus comatus - Shaggy Inkcap
- Coprinus silvaticus
- Ganoderma applanatum - Artist's Bracket
- Hygrocybe conica - Blackening Waxcap
- Hygrocybe virginea - Snowy Waxcap
- Hygrocybe persistens – Persistent Waxcap
- Hygrocybe psittacina - Parrot Waxcap
- Lactarius camphoratus -Curry Milkcap
- Lepista flaccida - Tawny Funnel
- Macrolepiota rhacodes - Shaggy Parasol
- Marasmius rotula – Collared Parachute
- Micromphale foetidum - Foetid Parachute

Fungi in Ryde Cemetery

139

Ryde Cemetery provides a wonderful green space and a haven for wildlife in the centre of the town. It is an ideal place to carry out nature studies with children, and a pleasant place for a relaxing stroll.

Beech Flowers 29 April 2006

Bay Berries October 2007

Photographs of many of the plants and animals found in Ryde Cemetery are available in the Nature Gallery of our website www.rshg.org.uk.

INDEX

All places are in Ryde, Isle of
Wight, unless otherwise stated

St Pancras Station, London 34
St Paul's Chapel 8, 11, 12, 18
St Peter's Basilica, Rome, Italy 47
St Thomas Chapel 28, 29, 31, 32
St Thomas' Church 32, 33, 85, 122
St Thomas' National School 61
St Thomas of Canterbury Church, Newport, Isle of Wight 47
St Thomas' Square, Newport, Isle of Wight 102
St Thomas' Square, Ryde 103
St Thomas' Street 27
St Vincents Road 76
Salter, John 11
Sanderson, James 29, 30, 32
Sandown Grammar School 71
Sandown, Isle of Wight 11
Sandy Lakes Farm 25
Sansom, Mr 65
Saunders, Charles 8
Saunders, Rev J H 51
Saunders, Tom 66
Schneider Trophy 105
School Attendance Officer 64, 65
School Board 62, 63, 65, 66, 67, 68
School of Art 68, 71
School Street 69
Scotland 113, 127
Scott, John Oldred 34
Scott, Sir Gilbert 34
Scratchell's Bay 123
Seacroft, Queens Road 128
Seagull Pavilion 96
Seaview, Isle of Wight 102, 108, 126, 127
Seeley, John Edward Bernard 37
Selina, The 119
Sellars, James Elias 11
Shamford, Isle of Wight 26
Shanklin, Isle of Wight 76, 99
Sheppard, Elizabeth 85
Shute, Emily 87
Shute, Messrs R 87
Shute, Mr 87
Sibbick, Jacob 64
Sibley, Thomas 10, 11
Sibthorp, Rev Richard Waldo 39, 40, 47
Simeon Street 98, 99
Simeon, Edward 72
Simeon, Sir John 9, 42

Sir Arthur Holbrook Lodge of Mark Masons 128
Sisters of Mercy, Abingdon 59
Sivell, Stephen 118
Skeat, Francis 37
Sloop Inn, Wootton, Isle of Wight 104
Smallbrook Farm 9
Smallbrook Junction 99
Smallbrook 25
Smith & Sons 110
Smith, James 10, 11
Smithers, Fred 65
Smout, Richard 6, 136
Solent The 44, 94, 112, 113, 114, 120, 122, 124
Somerfield 55
South Molton, Devon 56
Southampton, Hampshire 12, 15, 30, 76, 87, 95, 107, 122, 126, 127, 128
Southcott, Henry 118
Southcott, Samuel 118
Southern Railway Company 96
Southern Railways 99
Southsea, Hampshire 10, 51, 81, 90, 116, 119, 120,
Southwark Cathedral, London 58
Spencer Road 29, 85
Spencer, Countess 61
Spithead 24, 112, 124, 127
Squire, Rev C E 74
SS Bismarck 126
SS Imperator 127
SS Leviathan 127
SS Vaterland 127
Stallard, Captain James 129, 130
Stannard, John 9
Star Inn 85
Star Street Brewery 85
Star Street 68, 77, 83, 85, 86
Station Street 91
Stoke Cottage, 48 Star Street 83
Stokes Bay Pier and Railway Company 97
Stokes Bay, Hampshire 97
Stone, George 122
Stonepitts Farm 105
Strand Hotel 88
Strand 64, 98, 124
Stratton, William 9
Stray Leaves 74
Strong, Carol 3

Sturbridge House 73
Summer Street, Willenhall, Wolverhampton 77
Sumner, Right Reverend Charles 37
Sun, The 129
Superintendent of Chichester Cemetery 14
Superintendent of Police 11, 13
Surveyors' Institute of Ontario 71
Sutton, George 95
Swainston House, Calbourne, Isle of Wight 42
Swanmore Middle School 76
Swanmore Road 88
Swanmore 44, 56
Sweetman Brothers 85, 86, 87
Sweetman, Charles 86
Sweetman, Edward 82, 84, 85, 86, 87
Sweetman, Elizabeth 87
Sweetman, Henry 86
Sweetman, Mary 85
Sweetman, Thomas 85
Sweetman, Walter 86, 87
Symonds, Rev A J 54

T

Tasmania 116
Taylor & Co 34
Taylor, Joseph 65
Taylor, Rev J 55
Telford, Father John 48, 58
Telford, Rev J 11
The Baptist Record 53
The Bothey, Ryde Cemetery 22
The Christian Spectator 52
The Correspondent 72
The English College, Rome, Italy 47
The Foyer Project 55
The Freeman 52
The London Gazette 37
The Nonconformist 52
The Quiver 52
The Times Educational Supplement 72
Thomas, Bishop of Southwark 16, 47, 48, 58, 59
Thomas, Mr R P 41
Thompson, Sir Henry 71
Thorne, Mrs 54
Thurlow, Edward 9
Tichborne Claimant 78
Tichborne, Lady 78

Tichborne, Sir Roger 78
Titular Bishop of Thagara 59
Totland Bay, Isle of Wight 123
Town Commissioners 8, 9, 30, 97, 99
Town Crier 11
Town Hall 30, 52, 68, 75, 120
Town Mortuary 11
Town Surveyor 9
Tramway Company 98
Trelawney, Right Rev Jonathan 32
Trinity Church, Huntingdon, York 52
Trinity House 75, 128
Tristram, Rev W M 54
Trust of St Thomas' 33
Tub Well 27
Turner, Rev H H 53
Tutton, Mr 102

U

Undertakers' Arms 130
Union Lane 5, 105
Union Road 82, 85, 92, 100
Union Street 27, 28, 29, 81, 82, 114, 120, 122
United States Line 127
University of London 76
Upper Chine, Shanklin, Isle of Wight 76
Upper Grade Boys' School 71
Upper Grade School 71, 75
Upper Ryde 25, 27, 28, 49, 82,
Upton Road 50, 65
Upton Windmill 87, 88

V

Valparaiso, Chile 78
Vanner Family 104, 105
Vanner, Abraham 104, 105
Vanner, Jemeley 104
Vanner, Mr 102
Vectis Chess Club 79
Vectis Cycling Club 101
Vectis Hall 61
Ventnor, Isle of Wight 84, 104, 108
Vernon Square 53, 81
Vertue, Bishop 59
Vicar General of the Portsmouth Diocese 59
Victor House 86
Victoria Pier 97
Victoria Rooms, Lind Street 52, 62

Victoria Street 47
Vine Inn 122
Vines, PC 119
Volante, The 118

W

W B & C Mew 81
W B Mew Langton 87
W S Flowers, The 116
Wade, Rev A J 37
Wagga Wagga, Australia 78
Waghorn, Captain Martin 124
Waghorn, Henry 105
Wagner, John 8
Wagner, Mrs 122
Wales 128
Walker, Charles 68
Walrond Cottage, George Street 92
Walrond House 92
Walworth, Surrey 39
Wapping, London 78
War Department 109
Warman, Derek 6
War Memorial Chapel 35
Ward Lock's Guide of 1919, 34
Ward, Corporal Edgar 101
Ward, Edmund 101
Ward, Edward Tom 101
Ward, Eleanor 101
Warder, Joseph 11
Warne, Mr J 70
Warner, The 119
Water Bailiff 27
Waterloo East Station, London 99
Watson, Rev D R 51
Waverley Trust 115
Wearn, Charles 122
Wearn, John 122
Weeks Hotel 84
Weeks 49, 50
Welch, Charles 66, 67
Wells College 56
Wells House School, Malvern, Wiltshire 74
Welsh, John Kemp 50
Wesleyan Church 107
Wesleyan Methodist Chapel 101
West Quay 28
West Street 1, 4, 8, 11, 12, 16, 18, 19, 47, 64, 103

Western Esplanade 26
Westmont, Queens Road 29, 75
Wheat Sheaf 82
White Star Lines 126, 127
White, James 12
White, Thomas R 10
White's Directory of 1859, 49
Whitney, James 11
Wicker, Henry 49
Wicks, Miss 70
Wilberforce, Right Reverend Samuel 34, 45
William the Conqueror 25
Williams, Arthur 107
Williams Elizabeth 107, 108
Williams, George 107
Williams, Harry 107, 108
Williams, James 9
Williams, Private George Henry 107
Williams, Sydney Harry 107
Willis, Henry 35
Willis, Rev E J 54
Wiltshire, Mr 65
Wix, Rev Richard 45
Wood Street 90
Woodlands, Queens Road 86
Woodlands Vale 42
Wootton, Isle of Wight 104
Wootton Creek, Isle of Wight 115
Worsley, Elizabeth 26
Worsley, Giles 26, 27
Worsley, Lancashire 27
Worsley, Margaret 27
Worsley, Richard 27
Worsley, Sir Robert 27
Wrigley, Rev Hugh 54

Y

Yard Family 37
Yarmouth, Isle of Wight 26
Yates, George 81
Yates, John 81
Yelf, Robert 73, 82
Yelf's Hotel 82, 88
York Minster, York 48
Young Christians' Band 53
Young, Mr H 69

Sources

1871 Historical and Commercial Directory of the Isle of Wight

A Short Guided Tour of All Saints' Parish Church

Al Rowe

All Saints Church - Ward Lock's Guide 1919

An Emerging History of Christianity www.wightchurches.co.uk

Ann and Les Barrett http://members.lycos.co.uk/s0uthbury

BBC H2G2 www.bbc.co.uk/h2g2

Bishop Lovett Middle School www.bishop-lovett.iow.sch.uk

Brian Bosley

British & Foreign School Society www.bfss.org.uk/past

Christ Church (Baptist), Ryde, IOW by Rev E J Willis

Cunard Heritage www.cunard.co.uk

David Marshall

Haylands Primary School www.haylands.iow.sch.uk

Holy Trinity Church www.holytrinityryde.org.uk

Isle of Wight County Press

Isle of Wight Observer

Isle of Wight Record Office

Isle of Wight Times

John Harrington article by Patrick Nott, Isle of Wight Industrial Archaeology Society website
www.iwias.org.uk

Myths & Milestones in Bicycle Evolution by William Hudson

www.jimlangley.net/ride/bicyclehistorywh

National Society for Promoting Religious Education www.natsoc.org.uk

Official Isle of Wight Website www.iwight.com

Parish Churches of the Isle of Wight by Marian Lane

Put out the Flag, The Story of Isle of Wight Carriers, 1860-1960 by Derek Sprake

Roy Brinton

Ryde Baptist Church www.rydebaptist.org

Ryde School www.rydeschool.org.uk

Ryde to Rome by Peter Clarke

Ryde's Roman Catholic Bishops by the Isle of Wight Catholic History Society

Spartacus Educational www.spartacus.schoolnet.co.uk

St James' Church, Ryde - A Short History by Stephen Green ME

St John's Church, Ryde www.stjohnsryde.org.uk

The Chronicle of Holy Trinity Church, Ryde by Jack Wheeler

The Pedalling History Bicycle Museum www.pedalinghistory.com/PHhistory.html

The Story since 1948 (Ryde Baptist Church) by Martin Light

White's Directory of 1859 and 1871

Wightlink www.wightlink.co.uk

Wikipedia www.wikipedia.org

RSHG Membership Application Form
(This form may be photocopied)

Please fill in the form below, and send
it with your payment to:

Ryde Social Heritage Group
Membership Secretary
17 Hope Road,
Elmfield, Ryde.
Isle of Wight. PO33 1AG

Annual Membership Subscription £10
Please make cheques payable to
Ryde Social Heritage Group.
BLOCK LETTERS PLEASE

Title: Mr / Mrs / Miss / Ms / Other
Forename: . . . .
Surname: . . . .
Address:. . . . .
. . . .
. . . .
Postcode: . . . .
Phone Number: . . . .
Please tick if Ex-directory

E-mail:. . . . .

Ryde Social Heritage Group will use the information you have provided on
this application form for the processing of your application. We will not
disclose your Personal data to any third party or transfer it outside the
European Economic Area. We may contact you to discuss your application.
Your personal data will be deleted from our files no later than 7 years from
when your membership terminates.

(RSHG 1)